# Holding Hands with Pascal

# Holding Hands with Pascal

Following Christ with a Special Needs Child

BART B. BRUEHLER

WIPF & STOCK · Eugene, Oregon

HOLDING HANDS WITH PASCAL
Following Christ with a Special Needs Child

Copyright © 2014 Bart B. Bruehler. All rights reserved. Except for brief quotations in critical publications or reviews, no part of this book may be reproduced in any manner without prior written permission from the publisher. Write: Permissions, Wipf and Stock Publishers, 199 W. 8th Ave., Suite 3, Eugene, OR 97401.

Wipf & Stock
An Imprint of Wipf and Stock Publishers
199 W. 8th Ave., Suite 3
Eugene, OR 97401

www.wipfandstock.com

ISBN 13: 978-1-62564-170-0

"After Pensees" by Mary M. Brown originally published in *The Cresset*, Lent 2008. All rights reserved. Used by permission.

"Bound to Come Some Trouble" lyrics by Richard Mullins, copyright © Universal Music—Brentwood Benson Publishing (ASCAP). All rights reserved. Used by permission.

All Scripture quotations, unless otherwise noted, are taken from the New Revised Standard Version of the Bible, copyright © 1989, Division of Christian Education of the National Council of the Churches of Christ in the United States of America. All rights reserved. Used by permission.

This book is dedicated to my mother, Patricia.
She has said and done just the right thing for me so many
times that I have lost count.

# Contents

*Acknowledgments* | ix
*An Introduction (That You Should Read)* | xi

1. How Everything Started | 1
2. How Everything Really Started | 10
3. From Laughter to Mourning and Back Again | 20
4. The Best Thing Anyone Ever Said to Us | 29
5. An Older Brother's Burdens | 38
6. Two Fathers and Their Epileptic Sons | 47
7. My Wife Calls for Welcome | 57
8. A Father's Failures | 70
9. Holding Hands with Pascal | 79
10. The Gift of Pascal | 86
11. The Gift of a Sister | 94
12. The Gift of Weakness | 101
13. Where Everything Is Going | 109
14. Epilogue | 116

*Bibliography and Suggestions for Further Reading* | 119
*Scripture Index* | 121

# Acknowledgments

I WOULD LIKE TO thank my wife Anne for providing the initial impetus for this book and for continuing to read excerpts with heartfelt approval and healthy suggestions. The members of the Followers & Friends sunday school class at College Wesleyan Church in Marion, Indiana have been some of our closest companions on the journey of discipleship, offering welcome and encouragement through very difficult times. As well as being dear friends, they read and discussed several of the early chapters, helping me to frame the book in ways that would be more sensitive and useful in a church setting. My thanks also go out to Mary Brown, who offered invaluable feedback on my writing and gladly allowed me to use her poem in the book. Finally, this book is dedicated to my mother, Patricia. My list of thanks to her could go on for pages, but it will have to suffice to say that I could not be the father and the follower of Christ I have become without her love and example. Thank you, mom.

# An Introduction
# (That You Should Read)

YOU MAY HAVE PICKED up this book for any number of reasons. You may have a child with special needs. You may be reading this with part of your church. You may want to understand better how weakness and illness become ways for us to know Christ better. You may have thought the book just sounded interesting. However you came to this book, I am glad that you did, and I want to help prepare you for reading it. This book came from the very personal intersection of my role as a father, my training in theology, and my experience in Christian community. So, I want to personally welcome you into this book and help you begin reading it with this preface that introduces our family, issues of language and story, and my purpose in writing.

Reading this book will give you a window into our family. The subtitle *Following Christ with a Special Needs Child* hints that Pascal's life is embedded in the life of our family as we follow Christ together, and you will find that there is a chapter devoted to every member of our family, so it will help you to know a bit of our story. My name is Bart Bruehler. I grew up in northeastern Ohio and started following Jesus at the age of fourteen. I attended Asbury College (now university) and Asbury Theological Seminary. My wife, Anne, grew up in St. Louis and southern Wisconsin. We met at Asbury College in 1995 and married in 1997. She has a lot of variety in her church background (Baptist and Lutheran among others), but we have mostly attended and served churches in the Wesleyan tradition (Free Methodist, United Methodist, and now Wesleyan). After we were

xi

## An Introduction (That You Should Read)

married, Anne got her master's degree in applied linguistics from Ohio University in order to go on to teach English to speakers of other languages (often known as ESL). Then in 2000 we moved from southeastern Ohio to Atlanta where I pursued my doctoral studies in New Testament at Emory University. During this time we lived, worked, and worshipped with a refugee community located in the area of Clarkston on the east side of the city.

In 2003 our first son, Soren, was born, and then two years later Pascal came along. Anne's pregnancy and Pascal's birth were fairly typical, but at about four months we started to notice what we would later learn to be a rare type of seizure commonly associated with a genetic disorder called Tuberous Sclerosis Complex. Tuberous Sclerosis (sometimes abbreviated as TSC) is caused by the malformation in one of two specific genes that create specific proteins to control cell growth in the body. A disorder in one of these genes means that certain cells grow into tumor-like "tubers." They are not cancerous but cause trouble because of their abnormal size and location. TSC most commonly affects the heart, brain, lungs, skin, and kidneys. Pascal received a preliminary diagnosis after an MRI at six months of age, which was later confirmed by genetic testing. This began a steep learning curve for us: medical specialists, unusual medicines, therapy services, insurance technicalities, and other necessities. While life pressed on in my studies and Anne's work as an ESL teacher we also had to make many adjustments for Pascal. His health improved, but his development was slow and sometimes erratic. Pascal has visible growth on his skin and has had tubers in his heart and now on his kidneys as well. The most problematic ones are the many tuber growths in his brain, which have caused most of his health and developmental problems, including seizures. Early on Pascal was treated with Vigabatrin/Sabril (which we had to order from Canada) to help control his seizures. His seizures initially improved, but others cropped up and various treatments helped but often only temporarily. Anne, Soren, and I began to settle in to this somewhat unusual and unpredictable life with Pascal's seizures and delayed development.

In 2006 we moved to Marion, Indiana and Anne began training other ESL teachers as a professor at Indiana Wesleyan University. We saw this as an opportunity orchestrated by God. It was a great job

*An Introduction (That You Should Read)*

for Anne, closer to our families, and within a few hours of one of the best Tuberous Sclerosis clinics at the Cincinnati Children's Hospital. I was still finishing my dissertation, so I worked part-time and tended hearth and home while Anne worked. While I have had a variety of teaching positions since our children were born, almost all of them have allowed me the flexibility to be a husband and father first and foremost. After we moved to Indiana, Pascal's seizures grew worse both in frequency and intensity. He began to have multiple clusters of smaller, partial seizures throughout the day. Sometimes these would generalize into full body seizures that ravaged his little mind and were often hard to stop even with heavy doses of medication. In 2007, shortly after Pascal had turned two and after much consultation and testing, we decided to have Pascal undergo brain surgery. The excellent, wonderful, fantastic doctors (I really can't say enough good things about them!) at the Cincinnati Children's Hospital walked with us through the process. Over the course of two weeks Pascal had a grid placed on his brain, and then a specific area including most of his left temporal lobe was surgically removed. The recovery was stable and we saw very good results. Those cluster seizures were gone, but the surgery seemed to leave Pascal vulnerable to very dangerous seizures that would strike unexpectedly or when he was sick and required radical medical intervention to stop. Over the next couple of years we made several emergency room visits, and Pascal was placed into an induced coma more than once. It was a scary and stressful time.

After some failed attempts with medicines, we decided to put Pascal on the modified Atkins diet—a high fat, low protein, and low carbohydrate diet. This worked wonders for Pascal, even while it was awkward for us to manage as a family. He had a bad seizure while on the diet once when he was very sick, but he has been seizure free for over three years now. He recently came off the diet, and (praise God!) he has continued to be seizure free. As Pascal's health improved and the seizures were no longer a concern, we began to focus on other issues such as school and his speech and behavioral development. Several things came together that have been a blessing to Pascal and us. After several years of very irregular sleeping habits, we found a good balance of medication that helped him (and me!) start sleeping through the night again. Around this time, we also enrolled Pascal in

## An Introduction (That You Should Read)

Applied Behavior Analysis therapy. Through the intensive work with his caring therapists, Pascal has matured and developed dramatically. Finally, in 2009 God blessed us with our third child, our daughter Eleanor. While she is a petite pixie and Pascal is a big ox, they are developmentally very close to one another though separated by six years of age. I affectionately call them the "ya-ya twins" because of how they love to play and be together (for a while they would shout "ya-ya" at each other as a little game). The combination of diet, sleep, therapy, and Eleanor has helped Pascal learn how to talk, play, learn, and grow beyond what we thought might have been possible. Pascal is eight years old as of the writing of this book. He has come so far, and we have so much to be thankful for.

Telling our story of following Christ while holding hands with Pascal raises a couple of sensitive issues. The first one is language. A variety of terms have been used to identify and label people who face unusual health and development problems: impaired, retarded, disordered, disabled, handicapped, special needs, and others. "Retarded" has certainly left the domain of civil discourse today. "Impairment" and "disorder" stress the medical side of this experience, and "disabled" brings to the fore a lack of ability and function from a majority perspective. "Handicapped" emphasizes physical constraints placed on people by their (inhospitable) environment. Those who have thought through these issues have shown us that labels have the power to identify and then define a person—often in terms preferred by those doing the defining and foisted onto others.[1] Thus, changing the language and symbols we use can transform how we think about the issues faced by Pascal and many others, so we should choose our words carefully and purposefully.[2] I have mostly avoided the use of the terms "disabled" and "handicapped" except when they seem particularly appropriate to the subject matter. I have retained the use of "special needs" in the subtitle and throughout the book since it is recognizable and fits well with Pascal's experience as a child who faced several severe health and developmental challenges that we had to meet as a family. I speak often of vulnerability or challenge to reflect the fragility Pascal has experienced and the courage he has

---

1. Eiesland, *Disabled God*, 25–28.
2. Ibid., 90–94.

## An Introduction (That You Should Read)

shown over his short life. I have also tried to insert the language of differentness to stress how Pascal does not just have special needs but also special gifts, and the second half of the book will orbit around the idea of gift, the unexpected gifts that God gives to us in and through weakness. I have not found a completely unproblematic set of terms to use, but I hope that my language reflects my experience accurately, honors Pascal's life, and respectfully talks about wider issues faced by others as well.

I hesitated to write this book because I am regularly struck by the hubris it takes to say something about suffering that applies to others' experiences while making claims about the character of God at the same time. As I write, I know that there are other children with Tuberous Sclerosis who are still facing intractable seizures and behavior problems that have torn families apart. I know that young people face incurable cancer. I know that loved ones die too young. I am taking the risk of divulging my own struggles and reflections, praying that I do not further alienate or injure others who face pain that may be different from or greater than mine. Rather, my aim is to offer some sense of shared experience, solace, comfort, and welcome to those who follow Christ with their own unique challenges and difficulties. While I have also tried to ground my reflections in biblical passages and orthodox Christian theology, I know that my perspective on life and my view of God are limited. I want to say something that is true about God, his revelation in Christ, and the role of the Holy Spirit. I ask for the Father's forgiveness and for your forgiveness when I have not spoken rightly about God (Job 42:7-8), and I pray that I have caught and explained a few snapshots of our incomprehensible and mysterious God as the one who walks with us through our suffering.

Finally, why did I write this book? First, I wrote it at the prompting of my wife Anne. As we have talked things over and she has seen and heard my various musings and devotionals, she encouraged me to write them down. She helped me to see this was not a selfish project but a way for me to serve families who face similar challenges and the church as a whole. I mentioned earlier that this book sometimes seems to be a prideful risk to me. Anne helped me to see that it was also my humble responsibility to share these reflections. Second, I have written this book for families who, like us, have learned to follow

*An Introduction (That You Should Read)*

Christ with a special needs child. We have met many of these amazing and special parents through the years. This book is a small gift of encouragement, perspective, and consolation for them and for others who face the challenges of suffering and illness as part of their walk with Christ. Third, I have written this book for the larger church. I am far from the first person to reflect biblically and theologically on the experience of disability, suffering, and grief (you will see some of these authors quoted throughout the book), but I have tried to find a middle way between two types of books on this subject. On one hand, I have seen and read a number of short devotionals or very practical texts on living and working with special needs children. On the other hand, I have seen and read a number of thick and rich theological monographs on disability, theology, and the church. I hope that this book finds a way to express some of those theological insights in a way that is understandable to believers in the pew (or a Sunday school class or small group) in order to transform the way we conceive of the church and discipleship, for how we welcome the weak and vulnerable is an indispensable part of our constitution as the body of Christ. In the end, weakness is not an attack on human productivity but a gift that draws us closer to God and closer to each other, for through weakness we discover a Christ who was weak for us, a Spirit that fills us, and a bond that we all share before a God who loves us. So, I invite you to join me as we hold hands with Pascal and continue to learn how to follow Christ.

# 1

## How Everything Started

*And whoever welcomes a little child like this in my name welcomes me.*

—MATTHEW 18:5

This book delves into what it means to live as followers of Christ with a special needs child. Much of it will circle around the life of our son, Pascal, but even more it will explore our experiences while holding hands with our son. Thus, these reflections are about our life as a family. The story of our family begins with the relationship between my wife, Anne, and me. It is through our love and union that God brought Pascal into the world; it was into our home that Pascal came; and it is with our family that Pascal lives and will continue to live (perhaps for the rest of his life). The beginning starts with the beginning of our family. Let me share the story of how Anne and I met.

I had transferred to Asbury College in Wilmore, Kentucky after two years at another college in Ohio. I was trying desperately to graduate in four years and move on in my education, wanting ultimately to get my doctorate. I was taking a very full load of classes to try to make up for credits lost in the process of changing schools midstream. But after working constantly one semester with discipline and sincerity, I still found myself facing a huge assignment due the next day that I had not even started. With visible annoyance and grim determination, I decided to pull an all-nighter—something I had never done before in my college career. I worked all night and arrived at 4:30 in the morning with two results: I had finished my project on the gospel of Mark, and I resolved never to end up in a situation like that again. That resolution led me to stay at Asbury College one more year to enjoy my studies without pushing myself too hard. That following fall Anne started as a new student at Asbury College. Little did I know all of the ramifications that would result from that early morning resolution.

The fact that our paths ever crossed is a sign of the mysterious workings of God's grace through the people of God. I was a fifth year senior and she a freshman. As a transfer student I had become close to several guys who moved into the dormitory hall of Johnson 2nd East at the same time I did. My group of friends was more about where I lived than it was about when I entered college or what my major was. It just so happened (by providence) that Anne was oddly placed in a hall in a woman's dorm that had about half freshmen and half upperclassmen. Some of those junior and senior ladies were friends of mine and my other guy buddies. We met regularly for dinner in the "grey room" off the beaten path on one far side of the college cafeteria. We went to coffee houses and bookstores on the weekends, and we hung around campus and played games. We talked and dreamed about the future, often what the future would look like if we all stayed together. Those were good times, hopeful memories.

Little did we know while we were living that life and making those memories that God was already shaping us, directing us toward the path that lay ahead. Anne and I dated very little outside of that group of friends for the first year of our relationship, and we stayed connected to those friends. It was that group of fellow believers that placed the first stamp of Christian community on our relationship. We came to know and eventually love one another surrounded by and engaged with other followers of Christ. This trend continued into the future. I started graduate school at Asbury Seminary (just across the street from the Asbury College). A year later we were married. By this time some of our friends had graduated and moved on, some were more connected to other groups, and we now lived

*How Everything Started*

together off campus. During this time we became deeply involved in a church re-start with the Open Door Free Methodist Church in nearby Nicholasville. This fulfilled the role of Christian community in our lives for two years in the difficult transitions of marriage, off-campus living, and graduate school. We worked closely with a small group of people (mostly from the Asbury community). We became good friends with Bruce and Jessie Crocket and their two boys. Bruce and Jessie showed us what a marriage between followers of Christ looks like with its many joys and occasional difficulties. They shared life with us and so they became the unofficial pre-marital counselors who prepared us for and walked with us in our life together.

Our life in community only intensified from there. After we both graduated, God led us to Athens, Ohio where Anne began graduate school. She studied how to teach English to speakers of other languages (ESL) at Ohio University and we began working with Good Works, Inc., a multifaceted ministry to those in need in the Athens area. We lived in the "Hannah House"—a building that was home to us, interns serving at Good Works in a variety of capacities, and residents who had signed up for Good Works' long-term homeless recovery program. This home was also a hostel for guests who came to visit the ministry, especially including the Work & Worship teams, usually church groups who came to join with us for a week in service. If that wasn't enough, there was also an office and a store in the large rambling house. Good Works is a Christian community of hope that offers hospitality in a myriad of ways in order to participate in the coming of the kingdom of God.[1] We became a part of this community that intensely experienced the presence of God and the power of the Spirit—we worshipped and served together, we ate innumerable meals with one another, we lived and worked together, and we forgave and loved one another in difficult times. Anne and I often say that Good Works "ruined" us for most of the diluted experiences people call "Christian community." We loved and depended on one another in a way that consistently orbited around our shared discipleship to Christ.

At this point, I need to pause and backtrack just a bit. Sharing a group of friends was not the only thing that brought us together. First

1. See the moving call to hospitality as a Christian practice in *Making Room* by Christine D. Pohl and the brief description of Good Works, Inc. on p. 192.

of all, we were both geeks: we liked school, and we were both valedictorians of our high school classes. We both went on to graduate school. So, our first "date" was studying together for an anthropology exam. More importantly, we both shared a passion for serving God in another culture. Anne felt called to Bible translation and I to teaching overseas. Our time together at Open Door Free Methodist Church and even more so at Good Works enriched and expanded this vision. We still loved the beauty and profundity of the variety of cultures that God has allowed to flourish in his world, but we also came to see that mission was the very heart of God reaching out to the humble and needy around the globe. Working with children from the "projects" of Nicholasville, Kentucky and walking with the formerly homeless as they found healing and wholeness for a new life in Athens, Ohio became a part of this calling to mission. We came to see that mission was about weakness and difference. God took on weakness and difference when he became human in order to bring us salvation. God cares particularly about the weak and the marginalized in the world—those whom the Old Testament sums up as "the widow, the orphan, and the stranger" (Deut 10:18, Zech 7:10), and also the poor, imprisoned, blind, and oppressed who were the special focus of Jesus' ministry (Luke 4:18–21). It is then as we join in this mission that we recognize our own weakness and difference, coming into solidarity both with Jesus and the recipients of God's kingdom (James 2:5).

We moved on from Athens to Atlanta where I began my doctorate at Emory University. Atlanta is a large and daunting city, and we were at a loss for where to live and worship. God opened a door for Anne to use her training in teaching English as a second language with an organization that served refugees from around the world in Clarkston, a small but densely populated area on the east side of Atlanta. Clarkston became our home. We became deeply connected to several streams of refugees who also called this strange new place home. We knew several very sharp teenage Somali girls. We became close friends with a young Bosnian couple. We lived near and loved the kids of a family from Rwanda and a widower who had fled Iran because he was persecuted as a Christian. Then there were our many Sudanese friends who were so different from us culturally but with whom we shared worship every week—I can still hear their songs ringing in my head. Our church, Cellebration Fellowship (for it was made up of "cell" churches), had a few Americans in it as well. One of those Americans, Juanita Marks, was a nurse who moved to Clarkston to work with refugees and the church. She lived with us for over a year, became our dear friend, and joined our family as the godmother of Soren, our oldest son who was born while we lived in Clarkston. Once again, now living in our own apartment and starting our family, we found community and mission together, a community deeply interconnected and thoroughly woven into our lives as a couple and as members of Christ's kingdom.

This is a wonderful story of how God works in the lives of two people to draw them into Christ and together in marriage. It is a joy for me to relive these memories by retelling them. While this book is largely driven by the challenges we have faced as parents of Pascal, they do not in any way eclipse the joys of our love and the presence of Christ in our lives. Now I turn to describe how Pascal has caused us to both lose and to re-imagine what God is doing with us.

I mentioned how our experiences led to an expansion of our understanding of God's mission in the world, a mission primarily directed at those we might label as "weak" and "different." We believed for several years that God was preparing us to go overseas and serve as missionaries in another culture: Anne teaching English and I teaching Bible. We were just waiting for me to finish school and for us to start our family and then we would head off to wherever God called us. That calling, that dream is now on permanent hiatus—it often feels as if it is dead, a memory of a past life that we used to imagine but that can no longer be. Pascal's constant, intense, and ever-changing medical needs make it irresponsible for us to live and work somewhere that does not have the most accessible and up-to-date health care and medicine available. In fact, had we been overseas for his first few years of life, I am quite sure that Pascal would be dead given the life-threatening seizures that have rocked his brain and body on more than one occasion.

And so we grieve. We grieve the loss of a dream that brought us together, of a calling that gave us direction and purpose in life. This vision of our future life together as a family with God has not really been replaced by anything nearly so stirring and clear. We are currently following God in the dark. We hope and pray that we are making the right life decisions, but ultimately, right now, we aren't really sure because we just don't know what the grand plan is anymore. Sometimes we have pangs of doubt and guilt. Didn't Jesus say, "No one who has left home or wife or brothers or parents or *children* for the sake of the kingdom of God will fail to receive many times as much in this as and in the age to come, eternal life" (Luke 18:29–30)? Does that mean we should go ahead and pursue that calling of teaching overseas, entrusting Pascal's fate to God's providence and intervention?

Maybe.

Maybe.

Maybe.

In this difficult and liminal time, we just don't know. Not only do we have the burden of trying to understand and care for Pascal and the rest of the family, but we are not even sure if we are headed in the right direction. We have asked God hundreds of times what we should do: Stay? Go? Something else? God has been frustratingly silent.

One thing that has started to make sense to us is the idea of coming into solidarity with Christ and his people by sharing in their weaknesses and differences. God, knowing how important this is and knowing our willingness to serve him in this way, took that weakness and difference and planted it right into our family. We have come to understand weakness and difference as we never had before. Pascal is weak in that his physical, social, and cognitive development have been delayed and disordered in various ways. His fragile health has often put his life in danger. He is especially dependent on us to help him navigate safely through this world.

Pascal is certainly different. You can't tell just by looking at him, but his language and mannerisms quickly mark him out from "normal" people.[2] He introduces himself by describing his shirt. His words sound funny and mixed up, what we affectionately call "Pascal-speak." He is big for his age, loves to roughhouse, and he can throw the biggest tantrums you have ever seen, often at the drop of

---

2. Thomas Reynolds talks about the prevalent "cult of normalcy" that has the power to label certain physical variations as "pathological and deficient" while ignoring others (*Vulnerable Communion*, 60–65). While Pascal's appearance does not immediately register as non-normal, his social interactions place him outside of the pale of "normalcy."

a hat. He is different. People who know (and love!) us understand this difference and do their best to welcome us with it. Many others have found his difference perplexing, irritating, and even frightening. Thus, weakness and difference are no longer something that we have to seek out and come to know; it is as close as it can be to us. If encountering weakness and difference in mission brought us closer to God and God's people, having it as part of our family has done that even more.

Yet, this is no automatic result, for weakness and difference trouble us.[3] In many ways, Pascal's limitations, needs, and difficulties have separated us from the community that for so long was at the core of our relationship and our discipleship. Pascal is on a special diet, so sharing a meal with friends is no longer a simple activity. We have to plan ahead to have appropriate food for Pascal and worry that he will throw a tantrum because he wants to eat what everyone else is eating at the restaurant. We can't attend typical social activities like parades or carnivals. The noise and bustle either bother Pascal or, more often, make him so overactive that we can't handle him in public. His limitations make it difficult to go to church and nearly impossible to visit a new church. We can't just drop him off in a Sunday school class. He needs dedicated helpers (and thank God for them!) who can work with him through that time.

So, we grieve the loss of community as well. I often dream of having a front porch to meet neighbors, of sharing time with other believers at church, of getting to know people through our children playing together. Pascal's special needs hobble all of these things. He will simply run off (into the street, into a pond) if not constantly watched or in a fenced area, so a front porch would be a dangerous getaway. It is very difficult to have a conversation with our neighbors when Pascal repeatedly runs away from us. Pascal requires so much attention and care that I can barely say two words to friends after church because he is either throwing a tantrum or running away. Leaving the controlled environment of our home always makes me a little nervous because Pascal might do any number of dangerous or inappropriate things. Other children have a difficult time playing

---

3. We often fear what is weak or different because it has the power to reveal what is weak or different in us. Thus, we shun and exclude vulnerability to attempt to mask our own vulnerability (Reynolds, *Vulnerable Communion*, 110).

# Holding Hands with Pascal

with Pascal, and their parents feel awkward and apologetic because of their own children's difficulties with Pascal.

If the first half of this chapter was a bit too bright and positive, this latter half has been a bit too pessimistic. Not only are Pascal's weaknesses and differences gifts that allow us to know God better, but they can also be gifts that allow us to find a deeper and stronger community with people and other believers than we had before. Pascal's weaknesses and differences remind us, and others, that we are all weak and different, that God made us to need and know one another.[4] This has certainly happened in our marriage. Anne and I have come to know and depend on one another more than ever before as Pascal's challenges have driven us to new levels of vulnerability and trust. We have had to become more honest and more loving so as to sustain our relationship with the additional stress of a child with special needs.

The gift of weaknesses and differences in our family has surely been a mixed blessing. We believe that God has planted Pascal in our family (see more in the next chapter on this), but that does not mean that everything suddenly becomes easy. The grief of our lost calling and the uncertainty of our future overwhelm us, even as Christ draws closer to us in our weakness. We have come closer as a family out of the pressing need to support one another. We have occasionally bonded quickly with families who also have special needs children, but we have also more often felt separated from friends and neighbors simply because Pascal places demands on us that drastically limit our time, energy, and availability. In the midst of all of that difficulty, we have been hospitably welcomed by some who have taken the extra steps to not merely tolerate Pascal's weakness and difference but to love him and us. That welcome, that love has once again "ruined" us for shallow relationships, for superficial Christian community. We have been ruined in the best sense of the word, ruined for the weak substitutes that we often try to offer one another by experiencing the grace of God through relationships where weakness has made love truly Christlike.

---

4. Reynolds, *Vulnerable Communion*, 180–81.

*How Everything Started*

## Discussion Questions:

1. Read the context of the opening Scripture quotation in Matthew 18:1–14. Why is welcoming weakness crucial for our discipleship to Christ? How is this an appropriate quotation to open this chapter?

2. If you are married, what were the dynamics of your relationship that God used to shape your marriage from the start? How has God used these over the years of your relationship? How have they changed?

3. Have you ever had a calling or core part of your identity that God seemed to take away from you? How did you grieve that loss? How are you currently dealing with it? Did anything take its place?

4. Have you ever felt dissatisfied with shallow relationships in your church? How might our experiences of weakness and difference be the very gift to help remedy this superficiality?

# 2

# How Everything Really Started

*I will praise you, for I am fearfully and wonderfully made.*
—PSALM 139:14

THE STORY OF OUR family is one that has changed dramatically as we have encountered and dealt with Pascal's special needs, but our family story is only one rhythmic stanza in the larger epic that is the story of God and God's relationship with the world. Grasping our place within the cosmic currents of that ultimate story is both mysterious and necessary. It is mysterious, first and foremost, because here we humbly attempt to know something of the incomprehensible holiness and perfection of God. It is necessary because we humans have somehow been created by God to thrive on meaningful stories, and, as with most stories, the bigger the better. As we ponder how everything *really* started, I ask you to strain to keep in balance the frustratingly mysterious nature of what I am about to say (since there are no perfect final answers) and the pressing necessity of it (since we all search for answers).

Scripture, particularly the New Testament, occasionally points us behind the creation of the world to an infinite period before time began at creation when God decided and decreed certain things (e.g. John 17:5, Ephesians 1:4, Titus 1:1–3). More often the grand story of

## How Everything Really Started

the Bible starts "when God began to create the heavens and the earth" (Genesis 1:1). That first chapter of Genesis begins with God speaking into the formless and dark emptiness, the nothingness that existed (if we can call it that) before God started creating. Then God speaks and *bang*, things start to happen. The stages of the speaking-creating activity of God are punctuated repeatedly by the concluding refrain "and God saw that it was good" (vv. 10, 12, 18, and 25). This climaxes at the end of the chapter where God declares that everything made is "*very* good" (v. 31). Genesis 1 tells us clearly that God creates out of the badness of emptiness something that is good merely by speaking it into existence. Another very important thing occurs near the end of the first chapter of Genesis—the first command from God to humanity, "Be fruitful and increase in number" (v. 28). Reproduction is the first activity enjoined by God upon the pair of human beings. This pair made in God's image is meant to share in God's benevolent governing of the earth and all that is in it. Human beings (along with creatures in the sea in v. 22) are "blessed" by being commanded to reproduce and rule. However, it is here that everything goes tragically wrong.

You may think I am talking about the fall of humanity, the first sin of Adam and Eve, a disobedience whose effects trickled down to all of creation and to every member of the human race, and we will talk about that later. This grand story of the universe intersects with the intimate details of our family, because Pascal's condition crashes into a good world where human reproduction is supposed to be a blessing. What sense does a *genetic* disorder make in this scenario of life and creativity? A problematic variation in the basic fabric that forms our being as humans mars each cell of Pascal's body. At the moment of his conception, when sperm and egg met, something both microscopic and major went awry. We often apply the story of the fall to situations of inexplicable evil in the world: "Well, we do live in a fallen world after all." In certain situations, it is right and appropriate to try to rationalize evil by claiming that God is somehow not directly involved in the events that took place. Yet, it seems to me that something at the level of a genetic disorder pushes this fallenness beyond the horizons of our understanding. If something can (and did!) go wrong with the most fundamental created element of our existence in this world, the very thing that enables our reproduction in response to God's first command, then the goodness of the entire creation is at risk.

Another passage in the Old Testament intensifies this problem: Psalm 139. This psalm brings the macrocosmic creative activity of God in Genesis down to the microcosm of human reproduction (vv. 13–16a):

> For you created my inmost being;
> > you knit me together in my mother's womb.
> I praise you because I am fearfully and wonderfully made;
> > your works are wonderful, that I know full well.
> My frame was not hidden from you
> > when I was made in the secret place.
> When I was intricately woven together in the depths of the earth,
> > your eyes saw my unformed body.

This psalm begins with the declaration that God has searched and known the psalmist, and it closes with a prayer that God would search and know the singer again. Within the psalm, God's knowledge saturates the mundane, the extensive, and the intensive. After the introduction in v. 1, the psalmist relates how God fully knows all of the minutiae of daily life: when I sit down (v. 2), where I walk (v. 3), and every word on my tongue (v. 4). As Jesus would say, "even the hairs on your head have all been counted" (Matthew 10:30). From there, the psalmist moves on to the extent of God's knowledge: it stretches from the heavens to Sheol (v. 8), from the east to the west (v. 9), from darkness to light (v. 12).

Next, the psalmist turns to the intensity of God's knowledge in vv. 13–16 quoted above. Instead of pressing outward, here God's knowledge penetrates to the depths and origins of the psalmist. This intensive knowledge may even be the cause of God's mundane and extensive knowledge since this section begins, "*For* you created my inmost being." The psalmist almost completely ignores the facts of human reproduction (only mentioning his mother's womb once in v. 13), and attributes his creation directly to God: "*You* formed . . . *you* knit me together." The psalmist has captured both Genesis 1 and 2 here. He captures the fact that all creation lies entirely in the sovereign control of God (so Genesis 1) and that God is intimately involved in creation even to the point of getting his hands dirty in the process (see Genesis 2:7). The psalmist goes on to say that God not only created/formed his unborn body but was also witness to the process as well: "your eyes beheld my unformed substance" (v. 16). Finally, God's knowledge does not end at the embryonic creation of the psalmist but extends through the psalmist's entire life and to its very end (v. 18).

As with the psalmist, God's knowledge of Pascal embraces his daily life, the full extent of anywhere he might go, and the interlocking code of his DNA. The name of Pascal's genetic disorder is Tuberous Sclerosis Complex, and it is most often caused by a defect in one of two genes, TSC 1 or TSC 2, genes that control normal cell growth.[1] Now, it might be very appropriate and very comforting to claim the effects of the fall here: God simply was not directly involved in the misformation of Pascal's genes (other than perhaps by "allowing" it). I have many friends, particularly those who have endured multiple miscarriages, who have found that Psalm 139 simply does not describe God's involvement with the lives of their unborn children. But, I am trying to find a way to make Psalm 139 fit Pascal's situation, to keep God actively at the beginning of the story in light of his ongoing life. I believe that it was God who formed Pascal in Anne's womb, who knit him together. Knitting is an appropriate metaphor here, for Pascal's specific genetic variation could be described as missing a stitch (the cytosine base) in the fabric of his TSC 2 gene, and thus his cells can't control their growth quite right. God was the overseer and witness to Pascal's conception, knowing every detail of his cellular development. Pascal's genetic disorder is not the result of God blinking in a moment. Nothing was hidden from God, down to the "intricacies" of his formation (v. 15b). God knows about the entirety of Pascal's life, from his birth to his death. God intuits the kind of life Pascal would have, the challenges he would face, and Pascal's death is in God's hands. God understood all of the ramifications of the work that he was doing and witnessing when creating Pascal.

Embedded in this hymn to God's exhaustive knowledge of the psalmist is one brief but clear exclamation of praise that encapsulates the message of the psalm: "I praise you because I am fearfully and

---

1. For more information on and stories about Tuberous Sclerosis Complex, see the excellent material on the webpage of the Tuberous Sclerosis Alliance at tsalliance.org.

wonderfully made" (v. 14). And, it is here that I hear the psalmist proclaiming the words that Pascal cannot yet say but which his life pronounces very clearly: "I praise you!" "How does Pascal praise God given the fact that his existence seems to be marked by a mistake that flies in the face of the goodness of God's creation?" The answer lies in a more profound understanding of the rest of verse 14. Why does Pascal praise God? It is "because he is fearfully and wonderfully made." We usually take this verse as referring to the beauty and artistry of our creation, something that seems distorted in Pascal, but I think that it is talking about something different. First, the word "fearfully" here is a form of the basic verb "to fear" that is found frequently in the Old Testament. It often refers either to human beings being afraid of something frightening or dreadful (Gen 32:7, 2 Kgs 10:4, Ps 91:5) or to the human response of awe and reverence for God (1 Kgs 8:43, Ps 112:1, Prov 3:7). To be "fearfully" made in verse 14 probably carries more of the latter sense: the psalmist stands in awe of the amazing thing that God has done in creating him. This is an awe and reverence mixed with a healthy dose of fear, a sense of being overwhelmed by things above and beyond oneself (compare similar expressions in vv. 6 and 17–18).

The phrase "wonderfully made" is one word in Hebrew, and I think it is an unfortunately misguided translation. The verb here means "to set apart" or "distinguish," and it only occurs a handful of times in the Old Testament (Ex 8:22, 9:4, 11:7, 33:16; Ps 4:3, 17:7, and here, Genesis 14). It could by extension mean something like "to stand out because of its amazing character," but I think that softens the impact of the combination of these words and how they cause the praise of the psalmist. Let me suggest the following paraphrase for verse 14: "God, I praise you because my created being stands out in such a way that it generates a sense of gut-wrenching reverence for what you have done." The psalmist is so taken aback by God's activity in the creation of his very being that the only possible response is to praise the awesome God who made him.

Pascal certainly stands out, is set apart, is "abnormal" in contrast to most other kids his age. His behavior and speech quickly mark him as different. The problematic variation in his genetic code distinguishes him from most other human beings. The way Pascal was created sets him apart. The way he is set apart leads us to tremble

*How Everything Really Started*

at the awesomeness, the complexity, and the fragility of his life and of all life God has created, much like how the psalmist's own realization about himself led to the creation of the communal hymn of worship found in Psalm 139. I had no idea that two genes regulate normal cell growth in our bodies before learning all the details about Pascal's condition. Think of all the other complex functions in our bodies that are guided by the myriad of infinitesimal elements in our DNA! Pascal praises God because his very existence stands out in dramatic ways that generate fear and reverence for God. He bears in his body a special testimony to the creative power and wisdom of God. While he may not yet have the words to articulate it, Pascal's life profoundly and clearly expresses the sentiment of the psalmist: "I praise you, for I stand in awe of how I have been set apart." His life is a psalm that sings praise and leads others in praise as well.

At verse 19 the psalm takes what seems to be a surprising turn. After the stirring hymn to the incomprehensible wisdom and knowledge of God, the psalmist blurts out: "O God, destroy the wicked ... those enemies who take your name in vain!" The next few verses intensely portray the enemies of the psalmist as those who are also enemies of God and deserving of "perfect" hatred. But, this is not the last surprising turn in the psalm. In the last verse (v. 24), in what almost seems like an afterthought, the psalmist seems to realize, "Wait, I just prayed for the destruction of the wicked, and God knows me through and through. What if there is wickedness in me? Then I will have prayed for my own destruction."[2] The psalmist's eleventh hour realization relates to a late-coming realization of my own. I have prayed and still do pray at times that God will remove this genetic variation, this defect, this weakness from Pascal. I pray that God will "destroy" this disorder and restore to Pascal the goodness and rightness that characterizes all creation in Genesis 1. Yet then I step back and think that I, we, all have our own weaknesses, our own disorders, our own problematic variations. They may not all be of the same kind or severity as Pascal's problems, but we all have weaknesses that can bear similar testimonies to God. When I pray against

---

2. There are two different Hebrew words behind the two uses of "wicked" in v. 19 and v. 24. The first in v. 19 has to do more with guilt and offense (e.g., 1 Kings 8:32), while the second in v. 24 carries overtones of committing idolatry (e.g., Isaiah 48:5).

Pascal's problems, I need to be simultaneously willing to say the same prayer against my own "problems," and that gives me pause as it did the psalmist.

To close with a broader perspective, we need to turn briefly to the end of the Bible to help refresh our belief in the goodness God bestowed on creation at the beginning of the Bible. God is truly the all-powerful creator who makes things good, and God knit Pascal together knowing all that his slightly confused genetic make-up would cause. How can we reconcile these truths? Two subtle indicators in Revelation point us toward a possible, temporary resolution, but it is a resolution that flies in the face of how most of us conceive of life with God after Jesus returns.

The first hint comes from Jesus himself. After John is taken up into heaven in Revelation 4, his first vision of Jesus comes in 5:6 where the savior appears as "a lamb standing as if it had been slaughtered." In this inaugural revelation of God, Jesus appears clearly marked by his suffering and death. It is, in fact, his key identifying feature—looking as if he had been killed. We may recall that Jesus still had the wounds of his crucifixion when he appeared to the disciples after his resurrection. They were the ultimate proof that this was indeed Jesus, their Lord the Messiah (Luke 24:40; John 20:27). Why would Jesus still bear these mortal wounds in his new, resurrected body? Somehow the continuing presence of the wounds of his crucifixion and death are an ongoing testimony to his salvific suffering and to God's vindication through the resurrection. Jesus' resurrection did not erase the effects of his tragic death brought on by the sin of humanity. Instead those wounds are somehow incorporated into Jesus' glorified body.[3] Those wounds were a necessary part of the path that Jesus had to take back to his place of glory with the Father (John 13:1), and so they stay with Jesus, redeemed and ever-present for all eternity.

The second clue comes near the end of Revelation. After the defeat of Satan (20:7–10), after the creation of the new heavens and

---

3. Yong claims that Jesus' wounds are a sign that he has entered the human experience of weakness shared by those who are disabled or impaired. The wounds on Jesus' resurrected body indicate that our bodies may also carry certain weaknesses or wounds even in our future state of glory and renewal (Yong, *The Bible*, 127–30).

earth (21:1–8), after the new Jerusalem comes down out of heaven (21:9–10), after God and Jesus take up residence with human beings on earth (21:22–27), there is still a "tree of life" as well as leaves that are "for the healing of the nations" (Rev 22:2). This healing goes on in the broadest way for all of eternity. We often think that the cessation of pain and tears (21:4) means a return to a kind of pristine, pre-fall perfection. Rather, God takes all the wounds of that fallen creation and surprisingly includes them in the new, glorious creation. God does not simply delete all of those things that went wrong between the fall and the new creation as if they were a grand mess up that was a useless waste of time. No, God redeems all of the wounds, genetic disorders, and other pains of that era after the fall and knits them into the fabric of the new creation. Pascal will still have a stitch missing in his TSC 2 gene in the new creation and at least some of the changes that brings—only they will somehow be transformed in glory and worship. So, in the new creation the goodness of all creation is restored, the curses resulting from the fall are transformed, and they both join together to sing an even richer psalm of praise to God for all eternity.

## Discussion Questions:

1. Have you ever had an experience or heard of some horrible event that caused you tremendous grief and made you question the goodness and love of God? Describe that crisis and how you coped with it.

2. This chapter touches on the classical issue of *theodicy*: How is it that God is just and fair? Or, how can a good, all-powerful, and loving God allow evil in the world? What typical answers have you heard to this ancient problem? What new perspectives did this chapter offer?

3. Read Genesis 1–3, Psalm 139, and Revelation 21–22 together. This gives us a glimpse of the beginning, middle, and end of Scripture. How do these three passages bring together the large story of Scripture?

4. This chapter offered what I imagine to be unfamiliar interpretations of some passages of Scripture and an unusual view of the new creation. Are you convinced? Did you find the perspectives of this chapter reasonable and compelling? Why or why not?

I know there's bound to come some trouble to your life.
    But that ain't nothing to be afraid of.
I know there's bound to come some tears up in your eyes.
    That ain't no reason to fear.
I know there's bound to come some trouble to your life.
    Reach out to Jesus; hold on tight.
He's been there before, and He knows what it's like.
    You'll find He's there.

Now people say maybe things will get better.
People say maybe it won't be long.
And people say maybe you'll wake up tomorrow,
    And it'll all be gone.
Well I only know that maybes just ain't enough
    when you need something to hold on.
There's only one thing that's clear.

Reach out to Jesus; hold on tight.
He's been there before, and He knows what it's like.
    You'll find He's there.

—"BOUND TO COME SOME TROUBLE"
BY RICH MULLINS

# 3

# From Laughter to Mourning and Back Again

*There is a time for everything, and a season for every activity under heaven . . . a time to weep and a time to laugh, a time to mourn and a time to dance.*

—ECCLESIASTES 3:1, 4

*Blessed are you who weep now, for you will laugh.*

—LUKE 6:21

IF YOUR MEMORY WORKS at all like mine then you probably have snapshots of key moments that link to create a story from the past that informs the present. I have several of these snapshots surrounding Pascal's birth. I remember hoping with Anne that perhaps God would give us a little girl since we already had a boy. Later, when we found out he was a boy, we had to shelve our choice of name for a girl and return to the arduous task of picking out a boy's name. This had been hard enough with our first son, and now we had to do it again? I remember settling on Pascal Nelson Bruehler. We felt

## From Laughter to Mourning and Back Again

that his name should be of similar weight to Soren, who was named after the Danish philosopher and theologian Søren Kierkegaard. So we chose Blaise Pascal as our coming son's namesake, another philosopher-theologian. (Blaise Bruehler sounded too much like a race car driver's moniker.) In addition, we have a close family friend who has an uncle named Pascal. Finally, Pascal would be born just a few days after Easter, and Pascal means "Easter child." Nelson was in honor of my grandmother, Nello. Choosing his name was a meaningful part of our preparation for our new son. We had a name. Soren was excited about his coming baby brother. Everything was ready. We just needed our new little boy to arrive.

And arrive he certainly did. As many parents have found, the second child's birth is a bit easier. You have been around this block once, so you know what to expect. The first few months are still a blur of bleary-eyed lack of sleep, but a few things peek through. One of the snapshot memories I have of those early months is of Pascal rocking himself in his little blue bouncy seat. He would rhythmically kick his left foot until he swayed up and down, up and down. Soren was about two and a half at this time. He would run over and make goofy faces and funny sounds at Pascal, and Pascal would giggle and laugh. This was a delight for us as parents, and it brought joy to our home. We thought it was a good start to what we prayed would be a positive lifelong relationship between these two brothers, our sons. But then, something started to change. I am sure that it was unnoticeable at first, but in my memory I have created a moment when Anne and I realized that Pascal really was not laughing anymore. Pascal would kick and Soren would play, but there was no laughing. We had no idea why, though it is clear in hindsight. Our life as a family of four had a laughing start, but a change was to come.

At this moment between laughter and morning, we turn to look at Ecclesiastes 3:1-8, the source of the opening verse of this chapter. This is a short and poetic passage placed like a fulcrum between two tensely balanced sections of Ecclesiastes chapters 1-5. In chapters 1-2 the "Teacher" (usually taken to be Solomon) reflects on the futility and meaninglessness of life. Everything seems to be in vain (1:2). People work hard but don't ultimately gain anything (1:3). Both the wise and fools face the same fate of death (2:14). Chapters 3-5 step back from this brink of pessimism to find some meaning in life. Work and enjoyment are gifts from God (3:14). Friends are an important part of life (4:9). We must fear and obey God (5:1, 7). In between these is 3:1–8, a series of statements specifying that "everything has a season" (3:1). A look at Ecclesiastes 3:1–8 shows that most of the pairs start with the negative (v. 3, a time to kill) and end with the positive (v. 3, a time to heal), but just a couple go in the other direction (v. 8, a time to love and a time to hate). I think that reflects a basic hopefulness based on hints of God's grace, but it is not the only story. God has times for both weeping and mourning and laughter and dancing (v. 4). We were right on the brink between those seasons but did not yet know it. Very soon—too soon in Pascal's short life—not only did Pascal's laughter cease, but our family's laughter was about to turn to weeping.

Pascal had just turned four months old when his tiny body started doing something very strange. Again, I know that this started slowly and imperceptibly, but my memory now recalls his seizures after a point when they had become very frightening for us and for Pascal. Out of nowhere Pascal would lurch forward, thrust out his arms, exhale with a gasp, and then wince. Then, the seemingly involuntary lunge would happen again. These would come just a few at a time or in blocks of twenty in a row. When they passed Pascal would cry. Our parental instincts seemed to tell us that these were not so much tears of pain, but tears of fear—really, something much worse. The first few times it happened it was just something strange, and all kids do some strange things after all. Soren had a few fever seizures, scary but not very dangerous. Then these episodes began to mount in frequency and severity, and our fear began to mount as a shadowy gloom began to hover over our future, a future that had started with anticipation and laughter. You try to fight off that gloom. "No, it's nothing serious. He'll be fine." Yet in moments when God seems distant, uncertainty is near, and you know something is wrong with your child, it is then you begin to lose hope. You have not yet come to mourn. It is worse than that. It is the despair that exists between loss and promise. You know that something has gone, but nothing has come to take its place except a void of seemingly endless doubt and potential pain.

We went on for about two months like this. After the first few episodes we took Pascal in to see his pediatrician. Of course, he never had an episode in the doctor's office. We did get it on video a few times, but it did not seem to help bring about a diagnosis. Our very skilled and kind doctor initially suspected it was acid reflux, some digestive problem that caused him to lunge with pain. "Well, that seems manageable," I thought. But that was merely a false hope, a slender thread that temporarily seemed to rescue us from the void of uncertainty. Medicine was prescribed and more tests ordered. But the medicine did not help and the tests showed nothing—our thin thread had snapped. Being outside was one sliver of God's grace granted to Pascal during this period. It was a warm fall in Atlanta that year, and we often put Pascal in his stroller and walked through our neighborhood as a family. When Pascal would fall into an episode during these walks, they were shorter, less intense, and less upsetting. Still, the episodes overall increased in severity and frequency. Our fear grew with them, and my wife and I began to sense the loss that was coming our way. Joy without specifics can be naïve or simple anticipation, but loss without specifics is a gaping black hole that seems able to swallow everything. You try to let your trust in God distract you from it, but, somewhat like God, it never seems to go completely away. Other ordered tests were slow in coming, and we began to do our own research. Anne and I were sure that this was not a gastro-intestinal problem, but what else could it be? We began trying to search for his symptoms online, and this became our new thread of hope. It was a means of grace to be able to distract ourselves from the fear of our loss by being consumed with finding a diagnosis (and a cure). Ultimately, it was much less than the hope that we really needed.

    Then it happened. It was a Saturday. I had come home from a major event with my job that prepared college students to tutor older immigrants and refugees. Even though this event involved a hundred people and a myriad of details all in my purview, my mind was consumed with figuring out what was happening to Pascal. Anne was gone at another function, so I came home from a tiring morning and relieved our babysitter. When I had a break, I went to the computer and started searching for something, anything. I typed in all kinds of varieties of descriptions of Pascal's episodes, and then it appeared, a document entitled, "Infantile Spasms in Children with Tuberous Sclerosis." I read in that document the following description,

Holding Hands with Pascal

> Onset of infantile spasms peaks between four and six months of age. . . . Infantile spasms are seizures that result in sudden jerks involving all or part of the body in a forward (flexor) or backward (extensor) motion. At first, the seizure can be as subtle as a slight bob of the head or a thrust of the chin, but over time the seizures usually become more pronounced. Flexor spasms have been described as a jackknife motion, consisting of a head drop, bending forward at the waist, and sometimes pulling up of the legs. The child typically cries out during the spasms as if in pain.[1]

I knew I had found the problem. I just knew it. I knew deep in my soul that I had discovered *exactly* what was happening to Pascal: infantile spasms. Hope and fear burst together in that moment. The promise of something had emerged, but not completely yet, and the uncertainty of fear still hovered. I was waiting at the door when Anne came home, and I showed her everything. We debated for a few minutes but soon decided that we needed to take Pascal to the emergency room of the nearest children's hospital. We had recently captured one of his seizures on video again. We were sure that armed with these two pieces of information, something would be done for our son. Unfortunately, it was Saturday and a neurologist was not available. We would have to wait for an appointment on Monday. This sense that we had found something was another morsel of grace left by God to help us along the way, a taste of a fuller meal yet to come.

Let me pause at this moment in the story (as we had to wait over an agonizingly long Sunday) to point out a lesson for "normal" life that I learned from this very extreme process. You might have noticed earlier that I spoke of hints, slivers, threads, and morsels of grace. As I look back, I now see that we survived on these during the confusing two months between the arrival of Pascal's seizures and a diagnosis. This was an intense period, like walking through an unfamiliar and empty city block late at night. You do not know exactly where you are or where you are going. You are filled with uncertainty and fear. Your mental and sensory faculties are heightened, attuned to any change. It is a period of tightness and movement and stress.

---

1. This document is still online at http://www.tsalliance.org/documents/Infantile%20Spasms%20in%20Children%20with%20TSC.pdf

During times like this we must pay attention to our circumstances in a way that is so focused that God knows we need those little bits of grace spread out along our path. We cannot stop for a full meal. We are like the Israelites preparing to leave Egypt in a hurry. We do not have time for the bread to rise; we just need sustenance for the way. It is a time of fasting for the sake of the task at hand. These two months had an arc, a beginning and an end (which was a new beginning). I have come to see, though, that the busyness and multiplicity of our "regular" lives often puts us into this famine mode. Then the fast becomes the norm. We learn to live on a meager diet of God's grace, a diet God provides for us in the midst of crisis, but we seem to get stuck in the mode of thinking every task is a crisis; we turn crisis into normal. Having a period of crisis has taught me about the differing rhythms of God's grace and how we receive and digest it. God definitely provided morsels of grace for us as we walked through the ambiguity and anxiety of those two months of unidentified seizures. But as time stretched on and we were called to live a new kind of life as followers of Christ with a special needs child, our diet of grace would need to change as well. God will offer it, but we need to switch out of fasting mode to receive it.

Monday came and we went to the neurologist's office to see Dr. Flamini. Pascal was hooked up for his first of many EEG (Electro-Encephalo-Gram) tests. This is a long and messy process of attaching a few dozen electrodes to his head with sticky goo to help the connection. Yes, the EEG came out abnormal with a brain wave pattern typical of infantile spasms. Dr. Flamini administered a high dosage shot of B vitamins, which can cause this type of brain malfunction in rare circumstances. It did not work. We were told that it was quite likely that Pascal had a disorder called Tuberous Sclerosis, but a MRI would be needed to help confirm that diagnosis. We were scheduled for a MRI early the next morning—Pascal would have to be sedated for the test and could not have anything to eat beforehand.

We spent the rest of the day stunned, now in a different kind of limbo. We thought we probably had a diagnosis, but we knew not to jump to conclusions too soon. We did our best to wait, a waiting that banishes both hope and fear because it is so intense. The next morning Soren stayed with his godmother, Juanita, and Anne and I took Pascal to the hospital. Pascal received his sedation medication and was strapped into the MRI machine. I had never seen anything like this done to a child. It was done with kindness and professionalism, but it was still deeply disturbing to see my son hooked up to tubes and being slid into a giant machine. I have another clear snapshot in my head of the small, curtained-off prep room that we waited in during the test. There was a live video feed into the MRI room so we could watch what was going on while we waited. Now, I cannot remember how long or short it was, for shock and waiting have a way of erasing your awareness of time. I do remember Dr. Flamini returning with images from the MRI showing the lumpy white spots in his brain matter that was an almost certain indicator of Tuberous Sclerosis. Dr. Flamini broke the news to us with both clarity and compassion.

Then, we cried.

We cried a lot. We cried for a long time. We stopped crying and then we cried some more. The next several scenes in my head are all a blur. I remember a hospital room. I remember blood tests. I remember kind nurses and informative doctors. I remember lots of complicated logistics. I remember long talks with Anne. Most of all I remember the crying, the sobbing with Anne, over and over. Why did we cry? Why do we cry? We cried out of release. The past few months had been pilgrimage of uncertainty and fear, and now we had finally reached our destination. The journey through that wilderness was over, so we cried for the rest and resolution that had finally been granted to us. We cried because of the past. We also cried for our loss. We had been numb through fear and doubt and uncertainty. Now we knew, but the knowing was horrible. We now had to grieve the loss of something. We still had Pascal, but he was no longer Pascal as the healthy, laughing baby he had once been, and we were no longer the same either. He was now Pascal with the ominous mark of a genetic disorder. We cried out of grief for all that we had anticipated for him and us but was now lost. We cried because of the future, a future that would never be the same and that we knew would bear additional limitation and suffering for us all.

This has been a hard chapter to write, and I presume it has been hard to read as well. I knew I needed to write it though, because of the deep and consistent connection between grief and hope that saturates all of Scripture. Ecclesiastes 3:1–4 merely recognizes there is a time for both weeping and laughing, both mourning and dancing. That is true, but Jesus' announcement in the Beatitudes is more profound and broad, for he proclaims three radical points. First, Jesus makes a promise: "Blessed are you who weep now, for you *will* laugh." Those of us who weep and mourn in the present are promised a future that contains rejoicing and laughing. Second, and oddly, that future rejoicing and laughing results in present blessedness: "Blessed *are* you who weep now, for you will laugh." Those who weep do experience blessedness in the present on the basis of Jesus' word. In the light of the Beatitudes, the blessing of God is able to penetrate and persist even in the midst of the most all-consuming black hole of present suffering and grief. Third, Jesus is probably also saying that some type of weeping (or poverty or hunger or persecution) is a necessary prerequisite to future laugher (or life in the kingdom or fullness or reward): "Blessed are *you who weep* now, for *you* will laugh."[2] Thus, Jesus' promises in the Beatitudes comfort us in the midst of our mourning. Our present blessedness gives us new perspective on the past we grieve the loss of; we see that past differently. Jesus' promise of future laughter lifts some of the shadow of the future that has been lost when you realize that your child might very well not be all that you had hoped. The loss of the past, the grief of the present, and the fear of the future—Jesus' proclamation in the beatitudes answers them all: "*Blessed are you who weep now, for you will laugh.*"

## Discussion Questions:

1. What experiences of grief in your own life did you remember as you read this chapter? What pictures do you have in your head of those events? How did you respond to your loss?

2. When you think back to your own experiences of uncertainty or grief, look for the "morsels of grace" that God left for you along the way. What were they, and how did they get you through that dark time? Share them with the group and give thanks together for them.

---

2. See the discussion of grief and amazement in Brueggemann, *The Prophetic Imagination*, 116–19.

3. Describe your current "diet of grace." Can you identify different periods of your life where you fasted or feasted on grace according to your needs at the time? Have you gotten stuck in the wrong mode at the wrong time? How can you get out of the wrong mode and find the supply of grace God is offering to you?

4. What purpose does crying serve in our spiritual lives? Are you the crying type or not, and why? Recall a time when you cried and how it felt. What about when someone else you knew cried?

5. Read the Beatitudes in Luke 6:20–23. How does the promise of the future offered here by Jesus make us blessed in the present even if our circumstances say otherwise? How can we experience that present blessedness in the midst of overwhelming emotion and grief?

# 4

# The Best Thing Anyone Ever Said to Us

*To make an apt answer is a joy to anyone, and a word in season, how good it is!*

—PROVERBS 15:23

WE HAVE ALL EXPERIENCED the power of other people's words. They have the ability to confirm us, to deflate us, to unsettle us, and to console us. Most of us also know the confusing struggle to find the caring thing to say at the right time to those grieving. As the proverb says, "A word in season, how good it is!" Often, when we come to comfort those grieving (whether it is acute or chronic) we wrestle with our own emotion and fears as we struggle with what to say, feebly imagining ourselves in the midst of grief. This chapter is about how to support those in grief based on our experience of the best thing anyone ever said to us as we came to terms with Pascal's diagnosis and difficulties.

Oddly enough, the first thing to say is nothing. The most important element of comfort to parents who have a child with special needs is to simply be with them. This is crucial when the weight of grief that comes with such a devastating diagnosis first crashes into their lives. The birth and first months of a child's life are typically filled with joy and lots of family visits (and sleepless nights). However, that early exuberance can be tainted by the shock of a child's serious health or development problems. Friends and family often think, "I don't know what to say or do, and they probably just need time and space to cope with this shock." To that sentiment, I give a firm, "No." Now, of course, as with all of the advice in this chapter, you need to consider the specific situations and needs of the parents and family. No advice applies in every set of circumstances. So, with possible exceptions, I would urge you to go ahead and visit and be there with the family. Hospitals can be wonderful places where caring professionals work with the family and child, but they can also be lonely places, and a visit from friends is most welcome. That's what visiting hours are for. It may very well be awkward for everyone involved, but I have found I much prefer awkwardness to isolation. We will be considering the example of Job and his grief in this chapter, and here is our first connection to that story. In Job 2:11, Job's three friends hear of Job's troubles, and they immediately set out from their homes to visit Job and console him. They do not leave Job alone; they go to him, and they go to him together. The gift of presence and comfort arrives best when delivered by a community. If you don't know what to do or say when you visit your grieving friends, then take someone else along with you who also doesn't know what to do or say. Being together builds a web of comfort and support and eases the simple, mundane conversations that bring so much healing.

Presence and comfort does not end with the early days in the hospital. Most families that have a child with ongoing health or developmental problem caused by something like a genetic disorder or autism face a future of isolation and ostracism. That child may not be able to go to the church nursery, may not be able to attend preschool, may not have neighborhood friends, may be difficult to take to a restaurant or store. Pascal can often play too rough or throw disruptive tantrums at public gatherings, making us hesitant to go out in the first place or painfully embarrassed when it does happen. Similarly, Pascal has a tendency to ignore boundaries and simply walk away and disappear from sight, so even going outside to visit neighbors is fraught with risk. The demands of a special needs child can lead to chronic isolation: a lack of friends, a desire to avoid difficult situations, and obstacles to participating in typical community events.

So, make a habit of those visits, of finding ways to connect with the family in their new normal even as it continues to be awkward and difficult at times. The grief and struggle associated with a special needs child usually lasts and changes over time, and so the need for presence and comfort continues as well. We have been very blessed to have friends who tolerate all the difficulties Pascal brings with him (screaming, strange dietary needs, possible seizures, etc.). Also, our church has made it possible for Pascal to have the special help he needs so both he and the rest of our family can participate meaningfully in Sunday worship. Their presence and help has made the long journey with Pascal both manageable and even joyful at times.

Job's friends have something else to teach us at this point. Sometimes the best thing to say is to say nothing at all. Let's return to Job's friends: "When they saw Job from a distance, they did not recognize him, and they raised their voices and wept aloud; they tore their robes and threw dust on their heads. They sat with him on the ground seven days and seven nights, and no one spoke a word to him, for they saw that his suffering was very great" (Job 2:12–13). The first response of Job's friends was simply to join in his mourning. They did that in very culturally appropriate ways (weeping, tearing clothes, and dust on their heads). We each need to find the appropriate way to join in the mourning of those who are grieving a diagnosis and for those fearing what the future might hold for them and their child. As I wrote in the previous chapter, Anne and I cried a lot, and many people came and joined in our tears. They did not cry for us though; they cried with us. This is a crucial distinction. Parents bearing the burden of a recent diagnosis or long-term challenges do not need the extra burden of feeling they must comfort you in the midst of your own confusion and emotion. By your quiet presence simply communicate that you have come to be with them in their grief, to share in what they are feeling. Again, this has the healing effect of finding friends, the arms of God, surrounding you in the midst of your grief, and it fights off the harmful effects of fear and isolation. When our friends and family and church entered into our grief with us, we also found them bringing God's presence along with them— something that was very hard to find on our own in the dark times. It made it much easier to come out of grief into a somewhat normal life, a life that still included these important people even though it had changed dramatically for us. So, don't be in a rush to say anything. Just be there and love them by joining in their grief. This may seem interminably long (Job's friends sat there for a week without saying anything), but those whom you seek to comfort will let you know when it is time to talk (as Job begins to speak in chapter 3).

This book is dedicated to my mother, because she is the person God sent to say the best thing anyone ever said to us. At the time, she was far away, so we talked on the phone. I know my mom is a crier, so it was no surprise I could easily pick up on her crying over the phone. I knew she was crying with us, and it made my own tears seem more natural, more healing, and less painful. She said something over the phone, and she has said it many times over. It is the best thing anyone ever said to us, and it went something like this: "I know that this is really hard for you both, but I just have to believe that God knows what he's doing. You are great parents, and you will be exactly what Pascal needs."

I want to explain this further, but first let me offer a bit of a warning. Saying the wrong thing can add pain to the situation. If an apt word in season is so good, the wrong word out of sync with the time can be harmful. The power of words cuts both ways. God was not angry with Job's friends for coming to Job or for grieving with Job. God was angry because they did not speak "of me what is right, as my servant Job has" (Job 42:7). Their words both failed to comfort Job (cf. 16:1–3) and they misrepresented God (the two are surely interconnected). If you don't know what to say, saying nothing can be all right. Just listen. Let your grieving friends speak. Though it is hard, I urge you to avoid clichés, especially clichés about God's will and power. Some of the most difficult things ever said to us were the well-meaning words: "Don't worry. God can heal Pascal if he chooses to." Saying that always seemed to make light of our very heavy situation. "Don't worry," usually felt like an attempt to dismiss our grief before it had run its course of helping us heal. It almost made us feel guilty for feeling sad. Not only did it not comfort us, I think it also misrepresented God. Clichés like that were meant to give us hope, but instead they left us with the dull ache of doubt about a God who did not want to heal Pascal. This is a delicate balance to walk. We want to (and should) locate our suffering within the larger scope of God's will, but we are also trying to articulate something about our

## The Best Thing Anyone Ever Said to Us

incomprehensible God. Let me explain a bit about how I think we might do that by unpacking what my mom said to us.

First, my mom said, "I know this is really hard for both of you." She affirmed our grief and pain instead of trying to rush us out of it because she was uncomfortable. Often, we respond to other people's grief out of our own emotions. We are afraid of loss and grief, of disability and suffering, so we want to shut it out of our view, to make it go away. If you are going to comfort a grieving friend, take stock of your own emotional state. Be sure you are willing to look on the loss and pain your friends are experiencing and walk into that experience with them. There is a time to move beyond grief and loss, but we do not have to rush it. Especially at first but also during hard moments over the long haul, tell your friends the emotions they are feeling are normal. We do this by grieving with them first and then by what we say. Reflect back to them that what they are going through is painful and their response to that pain is completely appropriate. Tell them their pain is real and their feelings are appropriate. Don't rush the grieving. God has given us lots of examples of expressed grief in Scripture. There is a whole book entitled Lamentations and several lament psalms (e.g., Psalms 22, 42, and 88) in addition to the public complaint of Job (see chs. 6–7 and others). Embracing the pain of grieving loved ones will not bury them under the weight of their loss (sometimes this can be a concern). Instead, it allows you to walk into their place of pain and join hands with them so they can have the confidence to walk back out with you when the time is right. Facing our loss, mourning the loss, and embracing the pain are necessary steps toward healing and wholeness. Help your friends do this with your presence and your words.

Embedded in my mom's words to me was a statement about God as well: "I know this is hard for you both, but I just have to believe that God knows what he's doing." Here is where that delicate balance comes into play, the balance between saying something about God's presence in the midst of the situation without misrepresenting God. My mom recognized the difficulty in trying to find God in our present, difficult circumstance. "I just have to believe . . ." expresses both doubt and faith simultaneously. Her faith, like ours, was reaching out of our grief into the unknown will of God. She echoed our own faith's feeble attempts to place our circumstances within the broad boundaries of God's sometimes inscrutable will. She did not say God caused this or God permitted it; it was nothing that theologically precise. What she just had to believe was "God must know what he's doing." This was her attempt to affirm God's ultimate sovereignty colored by a recognition of the mystery of God's ways. This is not only a statement about God's sovereignty but God's goodness as well. It expressed our belief that the God who seemed absent was actually at work in ways that were good, in ways we could trust. Job's friends made a few missteps in their efforts to comfort their friend; however, they technically did not say anything that was theologically incorrect. Job's friends spoke solid and standard principles from the traditions of wisdom and Deuteronomy in the Old Testament: God punishes sin, and all human circumstances are under God's control. Therefore, if Job is suffering, it must be punishment for sin, so Job needs to repent of his sin to be redeemed from his troubles (for examples see Job 4:7-8, 8:2-6, 18:5-6). The resolution at the end of Job is not a clarification of the causes and reasons for Job's suffering, but rather a final statement of the wisdom and goodness of God and the woefully limited understanding of human beings. Job says, "Therefore, I have uttered what I did not understand, things too wonderful for me, which I did not know" (42:3). This is apparently what God approves of as speaking correctly about him (so 42:7). When we seek to comfort people, we should be bearers of God's presence and speak his name. The best way to do this is to simultaneously affirm that God is ultimately in control and that God's ways, while good, are often mysterious and beyond our comprehension. "I just have to believe that God knows what he's doing" said both in the midst of our grief.

My mom not only declared something about God, she also declared something about us: "You are great parents." Even though we knew Pascal's condition was not our fault and entirely outside of our control, we still felt guilty and inadequate. We were the immediate cause of Pascal coming into the world. We felt responsible for his life and could not avoid asking ourselves if we did something wrong, something that caused this to happen to our child. My mom's confidence in us was a reassuring "No!" to that lurking doubt. Also, in the midst of the grief and fear that I talked about in the last chapter, we really needed to have someone tell us we were good parents. Job's friends fail him in that they mostly criticized him (Eliphaz in 4:5-6,

Bildad in 18:2–4, and Zophar in 11:2–6) rather than supporting him in the midst of his grief. Who affirms Job in the story? It is God. God testifies to Job's righteousness and truthfulness (1:8, 2:3, and 42:7). My mom was the voice of God speaking to affirm us at a time when doubt, grief, and fear struck at the very root of our identity as parents and family. This word of affirmation was also a reminder that we were not alone. Someone else loved us, liked us. The current crisis in its gaping power threatened to separate us from all of our connections: family, friends, church. My mom's words reminded us that we were still welcomed, surrounded, and supported by others. Misery only "loves" company in a very selfish way, because it likes to have more misery around itself. In truth, misery is terrified of godly company, because that company offers the companionship and hope that can dispel misery.

Hope was the final piece of my mom's words to us: "you will be exactly what Pascal needs." Again, my mom's words directly counteracted the fear that clouded our future, seeming to shatter our dreams. My mom spoke a word of hope to us, and not a shallow hope. She grounded our competence as parents in God's provision—God had put us in this place and would make us into what we needed to be. She also did not make light of the situation. There would be real needs in the future. Pascal's life would be filled with additional challenges and threats that we had only an inkling of at the time, but God would make us exactly what Pascal needed at each turn. This was not merely a narrow shaft of light bringing hope shining on one spot in an otherwise dark and fear-filled situation. We suddenly had a renewed and larger sense of vocation from God. Job had prayed and sacrificed for each of his children before his troubles (1:4–5). That priestly role disappeared with the death of his children, but then it returned again when Job prayed and sacrificed for his friends (42:8–9). Our role as parents was now energized with the knowledge that we would be recipients of a special dose of God's grace, enabling us in ways that we had not previously imagined.

My mom has said something like this to both Anne and me on several occasions after that first moment of crisis and grief, and we have needed to hear it over and over. She has walked with us through several emotional ups and downs, always expressing in her actions and words a profound sharing in our pain and dreams. Her words continue to turn our hearts to a God who is both sovereign and trustworthy as well as mysterious and elusive. Her undying confidence in us and in our God has given us hope for the future, hope that helps us see our life and family as a special experience of God's grace.

## Discussion Questions:

1. Think about times when you tried to comfort someone in grief. What was it like? Did you feel at a loss for words? Did you ever say anything that you later regretted or anything that you found surprisingly wise and comforting?

2. What is the balance between God's sovereign power and God's mysterious ways? Why is it that we tend to emphasize God's power in the midst of trouble? Is this the most helpful thing to focus on with people in grief? Why or why not?

3. This chapter has referred to Job on several occasions. Have each person in the group read a different chapter in Job. What else does this book have to teach us about grief and comfort?

4. Review this chapter and identify the different ways that both actions and words play a role in comforting someone and giving them hope. Then build on this list. What else has your experience taught you about the power of actions and words? Relate some specific things that you can do or say to comfort people in grief.

I have one brother, Pascal. He doesn't look peculiar, but inside his body very peculiar things are happening. When somebody says handsome, I think of Pascal. He has dark brown hair. When I look at Pascal's eyes, they remind me of the deep blue sea. If you look a little closer you will see a few peculiar things: a bald spot on Pascal's head, a rough red patch under his left eye. This shows that Pascal has a genetic disorder called Tuberous Sclerosis Complex (TSC). This TSC caused seizures in Pascal's brain for four years.

Pascal plays enthusiastically, but sometime he irritates me. Pascal has a positive personality. As a loud person, he does not hide from new people, and he treats others nicely. With a creative mind, Pascal loves to draw. He is very intelligent, but sometimes he frustrates me. Pascal helps me in times of need. No one could ever replace Pascal, my special and only brother.

—"MY PECULIAR BROTHER" BY SOREN BRUEHLER

# 5

## An Older Brother's Burdens

*"Was not Esau Jacob's brother?" the Lord says. "Yet I have loved Jacob, but Esau I have hated."*

—MALACHI 1:2–3

*Since my people are crushed, I am crushed; I mourn, and horror grips me.*

—JEREMIAH 8:22

ONCE, ANNE AND I were invited to speak in a college class entitled, Psychology of the Exceptional Learner. We shared our experience developing an Individualized Education Plan (commonly referred to as an IEP) with the public school for Pascal. IEPs describe the special services and accommodations the public school must provide for a child with special needs. We talked about this for a bit and then the class began to ask questions, all kinds of questions. They began to ask about family dynamics at home, and the discussion turned to Pascal's relationship with his older brother, Soren (Eleanor had not been born yet; more on her in a later chapter). We described Soren as extremely bright, sensitive, a voracious reader, social yet

## An Older Brother's Burdens

somewhat awkward, talkative with a huge vocabulary, and mature but also prone to emotional overreactions. Comments from the class and the professor in the next few minutes made us all realize that we needed to talk about Soren in this class as well, for it covered not only children who were "exceptional" because of their special needs but also children who were "exceptional" because of their giftedness. Something that we had vaguely articulated before crystallized that night: we actually have two exceptional children—one with exceptional needs and one with exceptional abilities.

This chapter is devoted to Soren, Pascal's older brother. He is amazing in many ways. He took to reading almost instinctively at an early age. By the time he was seven I think we had read every dinosaur book in our local public library (both in the juvenile and adult sections). Not only did Soren read them, I think he memorized them. He spouted arcane information filled with polysyllabic words about dinosaurs and engaged in long discussions with our adult friends. He would conceive the most elaborate and technical plans for games and projects, particularly massive LEGO constructs. I sometimes feel like I am reading one of the bizarre visions of Ezekiel (see chs. 1 and 4) when Soren begins an explication of his imaginative (and somewhat unrealistic) projects. He has always done well in school and finds himself bored if he is not consistently challenged with new and interesting material. In addition to his intellectual acuity, Soren is intensely sensitive and aware. He is instinctively tuned into people and events around him, picking up on subtle cues and hints in ways beyond his age. Anne and I discovered early on that it was useless to try to hide anything from Soren. Whether it was surreptitiously suggesting to one another that we go get ice cream or privately expressing our fears about Pascal, Soren would recognize something was afoot and would begin to probe us with questions, seeking to pull out all of the pertinent details. His intellect and sensitivity combine with a wide range of passionate emotions. Soren can feel the greatest sadness and the most exuberant delight (sometimes more closely together than I can affectively understand). All this put together makes Soren quite a bundle of life and energy, full of questions and interests, always thinking and always feeling.

I'm still not quite sure why God gave us two boys who are both exceptional in such different ways. Soren will use his abundant

# Holding Hands with Pascal

speech for everything from playing to arguing. Pascal has made leaps and bounds but still speaks haltingly. Soren likes to build delicate and elaborate structures. Pascal delights in tearing things down. Soren generates complex make believe games. Pascal just wants to wrestle. Soren is intellectually advanced beyond his age. Pascal is developmentally far behind his own age. Soren is sensitive and has a wide girth of personal space. Pascal has a high pain tolerance and loves to sit on people's laps. Soren is tall and lanky. Pascal is big and stocky. It probably wouldn't take any parent's imagination long to conceive of the number of conflicts the two of them have at home. The most common tussle comes when Pascal wants to show his affection for his big brother by tackling him and Soren wants to be left alone. They have found ways to play together: trains, dinosaurs, and their favorite "run-around-and-scream" game (not mommy and daddy's favorite!). Their differences have prompted tremendous struggle and tremendous compassion in Soren. It is still striking to Anne and me how the two continue to coexist with love as both boys grow and change. We credit God with granting a special measure of love to our family.

Soren has few memories of life without his special needs brother. Soren was just over two when Pascal was born, and before Soren was three we had a diagnosis for the cause of Pascal's ongoing seizures. Soren knew that there was something wrong with his brother at an early age, but it was less obvious when Pascal was still an infant, and Soren played with and cared for his little brother with great joy. Pascal's early infantile spasm seizures were well controlled by medication, but another kind of seizure began to develop when Pascal was about eighteen months old and becoming a toddler. These "partial-complex" seizures only affected his face and head with an odd smile and a twitch of his chin; he stayed conscious but went into slow motion. As time went on, they increased in frequency and length, and we began to keep a "seizure journal" to track these and try to help his doctors develop a treatment plan. Pascal was walking now, and it was not uncommon for him to be in some part of the house with Soren when one of these seizures would strike. Soren, then four, would regularly come to report to us (or shout from upstairs) that Pascal was having a seizure and we needed to come and take notes on it. Soren has witnessed some of Pascal's most frightening seizures, has seen Pascal in the hospital between phases of complicated brain surgery, and has lived with Pascal's disturbed sleep patterns and inconvenient diet. These things have two divergent effects on Soren. They take a very real emotional toll on him but somehow have also dug a well of compassion in Soren's soul for his brother.

In his own precocious, ten-year-old way, Soren has struggled with the rippling injustice of Pascal's special needs. While we have had a lot of support and while we have made intentional efforts not to snub Soren in the midst of caring for Pascal, I know that Soren still feels neglected at times. That stream of emotion is small, but it can build up and burst out during times of stress. Like Jeremiah, Soren occasionally declares his complaints against the injustice that he feels so deeply (Jer. 12:1–4, 15:10–21). Soren in all of his in-the-moment intensity will say things like, "Pascal *always* gets his way. He throws a fit and gets whatever he wants, and he ruins everything for me!" These bursts hold both exaggeration and truth. Pascal does not "always" get his way (I have endured very long tantrums to ensure that this is not the case), and he does not "ruin everything," but Pascal has made things unnaturally harder for Soren. Soren is right that we do cater to Pascal's needs and desires more often, for Pascal lacks the self-discipline and communication skills to deal with not getting what he wants. He will either whine endlessly or throw a huge tantrum. We are painfully aware that we surrender to these tactics more than we should, but sometimes we are between a rock and a hard place. Many times, we have told Soren that we cannot go some places and do some things for the bare fact that Pascal cannot manage such situations. For a while, Pascal was fascinated by water and would eagerly try to jump into any body of water in sight. The biggest and nicest playground in our little town is right next to a (rather muddy) pond, and I only took Soren and Pascal there very reluctantly because I dreaded Pascal throwing himself into that pond. Thankfully, the city eventually put a fence around the playground, and Pascal grew out of that phase. However, similar dynamics have played out in many other scenarios, and Soren knows that he misses out on some things because of Pascal's special needs. It grieves me deeply when I know that the thing Soren is missing out on is me (or Anne). Pascal's safety and happiness require so much more attention, attention that I then do not have to give to Soren.

## Holding Hands with Pascal

Even more particularly, Soren has missed out on Pascal. Over the years, Soren has repeatedly lamented the fact that he cannot play with Pascal like a normal brother. Soren has longed to talk to Pascal, build indoor forts with him, ride bikes together, go down the street to a friend's house, and the list goes on. Nevertheless, despite Soren's longings, many of these normal brotherly moments have not come to pass, nor will they ever. Like Jeremiah, at times he feels desperately isolated (Jer. 15:17, 38:1-6; Lam. 1:1). Soren has wondered aloud in both grief and anger, "Why did God give me a brother that I can't play with?" So, Soren has felt cheated, cheated by God and by his parents. Oddly enough, he can share this experience with several other older brothers in the Old Testament. It started early with Cain and Abel. Cain was the firstborn, but God affirmed Abel's offering instead. Ishmael was the first child fathered by Abraham, but Isaac was the child of the promise. Esau was Isaac's first son, but he was duped out of his birthright and instead God chose Jacob. Malachi 1:2-3 picks up and extends this story to the nations that came from these two brothers, and God explains very starkly, "I have loved Jacob, but Esau I have hated." Then, in verses 4-5 God goes on to pledge to destroy anything that the descendants of Esau might succeed in rebuilding. No rationale is given. It is just the way it is. Soren feels a similarly obscure sentence of judgment. He did not ask for a brother with special needs. He did not ask to be the oldest son. He does not understand why God did this to him. We do our best to offer him love and support and maybe a few feeble theological explanations, but the wounds still remain.

However, our experience has confirmed the shocking biblical claim that wounds need not be damaging only; they can also be redemptive. This comes out most clearly in the life of Jesus (which we will explore in depth in a later chapter), but we find much of the same message in the Old Testament. Perhaps the most famous passage is the song of Isaiah, "But he was wounded for our transgressions, crushed for our iniquities; upon him was the punishment that made us whole, and by his bruises we are healed" (53:5). We are not sure about the original object of this song (was it Isaiah himself, another prophet, someone else?), but we see it resonate profoundly in the death of Jesus. The "servant" of Isaiah 53 suffers for the well-being of others through no fault of his own, and we see Jesus who bears suffering

## An Older Brother's Burdens

and ignominy for the sake of others. Similarly, Soren occasionally glimpses that his own anguish is a sign that he is the older brother whom Pascal needs to navigate through this world. Jeremiah speaks autobiographically about his grief as cited at the beginning of this chapter, "Since my people are crushed, I am crushed; I mourn and horror grips me" (8:22). Jeremiah perceives the reality of the coming military judgment on Jerusalem and he is physically shaken by grief (4:19). God tells Jeremiah not to cry or pray for the people, but in his deep connection to his people (7:16; 14:11) he persists in interceding for them (14:19-22; 32:16-25). Similarly, the people of Israel reject Moses and God, yet Moses continues to plead for God to have mercy on them (Ex 32:1-14; Num 14:1-25). We might think the suffering of the servant, the persecution of Jeremiah, and the rejection of Moses would effectively stifle any inclination they might have had to pray for or aid God's people. However, it seems to do much the opposite. The emotional experiences of these prophets make them even better intercessors; it only fuels the fires of their compassion.

Anne and I prayed early on that God would somehow use our sons' relationship for the good of both of them. Pascal has clearly benefitted by having an older brother who learns with him, looks out for him, and laughs with him, but it is more complicated for Soren. Soren can overreact when he believes Pascal is getting special treatment. He has felt neglected when Pascal's medical needs consumed our attention. He can be overwhelmed with his own confusion and grief over Pascal's difficulties. However, as with the prophets of the Old Testament, Soren's sensitivity and pain has also helped him develop extraordinary care and concern. Both boys were briefly at the same elementary school when Pascal started kindergarten and Soren was in second grade. This setting was not working well for Pascal and he would regularly throw loud tantrums. Soren could hear him but was not allowed to go to his brother (he really can help Pascal out of a tantrum), and this troubled Soren deeply. He was able to help his brother; he *wanted* to help his brother. This past school year Soren's class did projects on what dreams they wanted to achieve—in honor of Martin Luther King Jr.—when they grow up. Soren's dream was to be a pediatrician and find a cure for Tuberous Sclerosis. He is still a ways from choosing that life direction, but it speaks to his care and concern for Pascal. Soren has befriended classmates who have learning and developmental challenges (though not quite as severe as Pascal's). He recognizes needs and acts to help. Soren and Pascal still have their very obvious differences and sibling scuffles are a common occurrence, but the experience of suffering together with Pascal has built a bond between the two brothers, a bond that pulsates with vital compassion. Now Soren's compassion spills over into practical acts of care for Pascal and others.

I have often evaluated Soren's sensitivity as a burden for him to bear—to be flooded with thought and emotion and overwhelmed in their midst. It is a burden for us as parents seeking some equilibrium in a home with such radically different brothers driven to extremes by divergent causes. Yet, I have come to see that Soren's gift is the gift of many of the Old Testament prophets. The references to the prophets throughout this chapter are no accident. Soren reflects their words and actions in many ways, and I have come to see Soren's sensitivity as the key to a prophetic vocation. Prophets are sensitive to the word of God; they hear God speaking when no one else seems to perceive (Zech 1:1). Prophets are sensitive to the heart of God; they feel God's pain and are invited into God's experience with Israel (Hos 3:1–5). Prophets are sensitive to the plight of the needy, the voiceless whom few others hear (Amos 2:6–8). Prophets are sensitive to their people (Jer 8:22), and they sum up the corporate failure and repentance of God's people and present it to God (Is 6:1–5). God seems to have granted that sensitivity to Soren and then put it through especially hard training by having a brother who both frustrates him and prompts him to care. I believe that God will use this gift of sensitivity to enable Soren to sense the movement of God's Spirit, to perceive the plight of those around him, and to experience the pain of people who need someone to bear it to God on their behalf.

## Discussion Questions:

1. Read Jeremiah 15 and put yourself in Jeremiah's place. What has God told Jeremiah to say? How does Jeremiah respond and why? What then does God say in reply?

*An Older Brother's Burdens*

2. Choose one of your favorite prophets from the Old Testament. How does that prophet demonstrate the gift of sensitivity? How does it shape that prophet's calling and words?

3. Has anyone ever caused you to feel both compassion and frustration, both concern and indignation? Describe the situation and reflect on how it is possible to feel such different reactions simultaneously. How did God use that response?

4. Have you had to care for someone close to you with needs that seemed like they might overwhelm you? How did you respond? How did God help you through that situation?

When they came to the disciples, they saw a great crowd around them, and some scribes arguing with them. When the whole crowd saw him, they were immediately overcome with awe, and they ran forward to greet him. He asked them, "What are you arguing about with them?" Someone from the crowd answered him, "Teacher, I brought you my son; he has a spirit that makes him unable to speak; and whenever it seizes him, it dashes him down; and he foams and grinds his teeth and becomes rigid; and I asked your disciples to cast it out, but they could not do so." He answered them, "You faithless generation, how much longer must I be among you? How much longer must I put up with you? Bring him to me." And they brought the boy to him. When the spirit saw him, immediately it convulsed the boy, and he fell on the ground and rolled about, foaming at the mouth. Jesus asked the father, "How long has this been happening to him?" And he said, "From childhood. It has often cast him into the fire and into the water, to destroy him; but if you are able to do anything, have pity on us and help us." Jesus said to him, "If you are able!—All things can be done for the one who believes." Immediately the father of the child cried out, "I believe; help my unbelief!" When Jesus saw that a crowd came running together, he rebuked the unclean spirit, saying to it, "You spirit that keeps this boy from speaking and hearing, I command you, come out of him, and never enter him again!" After crying out and convulsing him terribly, it came out, and the boy was like a corpse, so that most of them said, "He is dead." But Jesus took him by the hand and lifted him up, and he was able to stand. When he had entered the house, his disciples asked him privately, "Why could we not cast it out?" He said to them, "This kind can come out only through prayer."

—MARK 9:14–29

# 6

# Two Fathers and Their Epileptic Sons

*Many times it has thrown him into a fire or into the water, trying to kill him; but if you can do anything, please have pity on us and help us.*

—MARK 9:22

FROM THE VERY BEGINNING of Pascal's seizures my mind would recall the story of Jesus healing the epileptic boy (see Mark 9:14-29 as well as Matthew 17:14-21 and Luke 9:37-43). In many ways, however, the story was too painful to think about. I knew the story attributed the boy's seizures to a "mute spirit," and I believed Pascal's symptoms and condition were not due to demonic activity. I also knew that Jesus healed this boy, but Pascal's seizures continued on and even became more life threatening. Nevertheless, I knew one day I would need to read this story and read it closely and personally. This chapter contains my studied reflections on this story, primarily using the version found in Mark's gospel. As I began to study this vignette, I quickly discovered that the story features the experience and advocacy of the father before Jesus, much as this book contains my spiritual reflections on holding hands with Pascal as we walk with Jesus.

## Holding Hands with Pascal

Mark frames this story by featuring the failures of the disciples in 9:14-16 and 28-29. This is a recurring theme in Mark 8:22—10:52. Over and over, the disciples fail to understand the true identity and mission of Jesus. Jesus has come to serve, suffer, and die, and the disciples just don't get it (see 8:33, 9:38-39, 10:13-14, and 10:42-45). The story of this father and his boy opens as Jesus and his three closest disciples are coming down from the mountain where Jesus was transfigured in the presence of God. Immediately on the heels of this high point, Jesus discovers the rest of his disciples squabbling with some Jewish teachers in the midst of a curious crowd (v. 16). Upon Jesus' return, the crowd throngs around him, but Jesus intently inquires of his disciples: "What are you arguing about with them?" At this point, the father of the boy, standing in the midst of the crowd, unexpectedly speaks up and lays the entire case out before Jesus: "Teacher, I brought my son to you because he has a spirit that makes him unable to speak. Whenever it overtakes him, it knocks him over—he foams at the mouth, grinds his teeth, and becomes rigid. I asked your disciples to cast it out, but they were not able to" (vv. 17-18).

The father is very direct. He brings his son to Jesus. He has taken the initiative to seek out the renowned teacher and healer. In Jesus' absence he presents his son to the disciples who cannot help the boy, in step with their recurring failures in this section of Mark. In verse 17 the father clearly identifies the cause of his son's condition. Oddly, it is a spirit that makes him unable to speak (more on this later). What stands out here is the addition of verse 18. Here the father provides Jesus with a full clinical description of the effects of the spirit on his son. What we find here is a specialized set of unusual vocabulary. The father states that the spirit "overtakes" his son. This is the only place where this particular verb appears in Mark's gospel. He goes on to add specifics. The spirit "knocks him over" (only used in a very different sense by Mark in 2:22). The boy "foams at the mouth" and "grinds his teeth." This story in Mark is the only place in the entire New Testament where these two Greek verbs appear. Finally, "he becomes rigid," a meaning that is not associated with this verb anywhere else in the New Testament. (It usually means to wither or dry up as it does in Mark 11:20.) This father is an expert in his son's condition. He has intensely and emotionally witnessed the

## Two Fathers and Their Epileptic Sons

spirit's attacks on his son, and he has refined this depiction over several heart-wrenching episodes. Likewise, I found that I had become an expert in Pascal's condition and symptoms. As we sought in vain for a diagnosis of his early infantile spasms, I honed my description of his seizures in the hopes that some doctor would be able to identify what I had seen take over Pascal's body. I became a professional at providing doctors with a prioritized and succinct explanation of Pascal's condition under emergency situations. After one particularly dangerous seizure had passed a doctor asked me if I was a doctor. She was so impressed by my command of specialized medical vocabulary and diagnostic criteria that she assumed I had formal medical training. No, like the father in the story, this is a specialization driven by love and concern for the well-being of my son, a specialization developed over the agony of watching repeated seizures overtake my son.

Next comes one of my initial stumbling blocks in this story. Immediately after the father's impassioned presentation, Jesus exclaims, "O faithless generation, how much longer will I be with you! How much longer must I put up with you!" As one emotionally involved in this story, I instinctively applied Jesus' words to the father in the story and to myself. Jesus appears to rebuke the faithlessness of the father right after the father has poured his heart out to him. However, I do not think that is the case for several reasons. First, Jesus answers "them" and commands the disciples (not the father) to bring the boy to him (the words here are plural, not singular). Second, Jesus goes on in verse 21 to engage the father in further conversation. Third, this comment fits best into the recurring theme of the failure of the disciples that appears throughout this section and this story. I admit that I have felt Jesus' consternation with doctors who don't seem to listen to me, with well-meaning Christians who tell me to believe God will heal Pascal, and with onlookers who scoff at Pascal's difficult behavior. As Jesus does, I pray I will not just complain about these situations but go on to intervene in redemptive ways.

When the boy is brought within eyeshot of Jesus (where has the boy been up until now? Biblical stories often don't fill in these details for us) the spirit immediately causes a seizure, the boy falls to the ground, rolls around (another rare Greek verb), and foams at the mouth. One issue that stands out in this story is that throughout the narrative, the spirit is the subject of the verbs and the boy is an object under its influence. It starts back in verse 18 where the spirit "overtakes" the boy. It continues here as the spirit induces a seizure, and it continues later in the story when the spirit (not the boy) cries out and convulses severely (v. 25). Analogous to the oppressed experience of this boy, I have often felt that Pascal was a prisoner of his genetic disorder. We sometimes see moments when an unshackled Pascal shines through with joy and connection, but we have many others when the effects of his disorder seem to be in control of his behavior with tantrums and confusion. Most of the time, he presses on through a cloudy combination of the two. But when Pascal is enduring a seizure, it is painfully clear his disorder is completely in control even to the point where his body and brain often cannot break out of the episode without extreme medical intervention.

Something very strange happens at this point in the story. After the onset of the seizure, Jesus does not immediately rebuke the spirit out of mercy for the boy. Instead, he engages the father in a conversation about the boy's condition. This dialogue continues through verse 24 and appears to break off only because of the intruding crowd. In the midst of the boy rolling on the ground and foaming at the mouth, Jesus, who can supernaturally perceive people's thoughts (see Mark 2:8), asks the father for basic information: "How long has this been happening to him?" The father responds, "Since childhood." Pascal's seizures started when he was just an infant of four months, perhaps even earlier than this boy. We do not know how old the boy is at this point, but clearly he, like Pascal, has dealt with seizures over several years of his young life. Later in childhood, Pascal was subject to very long and severe seizures (known as "status epilepticus"). I remember having several critical conversations with doctors and nurses while Pascal lay on the bed next to me in the midst of an uncontrollable seizure. As I read this story from the outside this conversation seems silly. "Just heal the poor child," I think. I know that when I faced similar circumstances time seemed suspended and my tunnel-vision focus on Pascal churned out what I believed to be crucial data about his condition to doctors who could help.

Thus again, the father does not stop with the basic response to Jesus' question, but he goes on in verse 22 to explain the situation further to Jesus: "And it [the spirit] often even tries to throw him into a fire or into the water in order to destroy him." Pascal had a few

## Two Fathers and Their Epileptic Sons

life-threatening behaviors like this. As a toddler and young child he was fascinated with water. Whenever we were in the vicinity of a pool or a pond I would have to watch him diligently because he would escape and try to jump in the water. Of course, he could not swim at all, so falling in a pool unnoticed might have "destroyed him." While he never had a fascination with fire, he faced the peculiarly modern danger of running into the street. Pascal had no sense of oncoming cars and would often bolt into the street unexpectedly. My grip became very strong as I held onto his hand attentively whenever we walked through a parking lot or down a sidewalk. I was fighting against the unpredictable rush of Pascal's disorder that often seemed to overcome his self-control and "throw" him into traffic or into the water. Many times, much like this father, I reviewed in my mind the scenarios that could lead to Pascal's accidental death. It was a real and present fear that I played over and over in my head partially because fear grips one in that way and partially because I hoped that I could anticipate and avoid such potential hazards. Keeping these things bottled inside, however, only exacerbates the unhealthy anxiety. Because of the prompting of Jesus' question, the father gushes out his deepest fears for his son's life, much as I did with friends who would listen.

Next, the father blurts out, "But if you are able to do anything, then please have compassion on us and help us." The father speaks out of desperation. His son has faced the destructive power of this spirit for most of his life and he is currently rolling around on the ground in the midst of a seizure. The father's statement does not cast doubt on Jesus' willingness but on Jesus' ability. I would add, in the father's defense, that this is not so much the father's assessment of Jesus' ability but a reflection of his own (and anyone else's) inability to do anything for his son over the years that this spirit has oppressed them. At this point, the father will take "anything," anything at all that might relieve his son even partially. If Jesus can do anything, then he ought to have compassion on them and help them (the "then" part of this statement is in the form of a polite command in Greek). The word for "compassion" is a fascinating example of how we associate emotion with parts of our bodies—our faces flush with anger, our hearts burn with love. For many ancient Mediterranean cultures, compassion or pity was felt in the "guts." The word for compassion here refers to our internal organs, what we might label "bowels" or "entrails," but especially the stomach and intestines. This is a profound emotion in the pit of our stomach that prompts one to act, and even God feels mercy in this way (see Luke 1:78). Mark has already told us that Jesus is frequently "moved with compassion" and then acts to heal people (see 1:41, 6:34, and 8:2), so the father's desperate cry for help sparks hope for the audience of Mark's gospel. And, this is not just hope for the healing of the boy (still having a seizure) but for "us"—"please have compassion on us and help us." While the spirit only possesses this child and while Pascal is the only one in our family with this disorder, the effects of their conditions spill over onto the entire family. Whatever Jesus can do, he does it for the son, for his father, and for their entire family and community.

Jesus takes issue with the father's formulation and its burden of responsibility. "If you are able," he begins, but then he breaks off and concludes, "All things are possible for the one who believes" (v. 23). Jesus redirects the issue away from his own ability to the possibilities that open up for the one who believes. The obstacles do not lie primarily with Jesus' willingness or ability, but with our openness to the activity of God in our lives. Now, we need to draw a careful theological nuance here. Jesus' response does not say that if you believe then all good things will happen for you. He says that if you believe then all good things can happen for you. A person's faith does not cause the fulfillment of all of one's desires or the delivery of all blessings. Instead, a person's faith opens the way for God to intervene as God sees fit. In the case of this boy and as a manifestation of his proclamation of the kingdom of God, Jesus exorcizes the demon and heals the boy. In our case, and for many others, God acts in different ways, and we continue to walk through life with Pascal's disorder. Jesus' response strikes a nerve, and "immediately the father of the boy cried out and began to say, 'I believe! Help my lack of faith!'" (v. 24). That healing for the entire family emerges subtly here, for the father "cries out" here just as the demon (and boy?) "cries out" when Jesus rebukes it in verse 26. Crying out and healing go together for both the father and his son. The father asked Jesus "please help us" in verse 22, and now he personalizes that request to "help my lack of faith." The father's assertion reminds us that belief/faith is rarely a black-and-white issue. In the same breath, the father boldly declares

## Two Fathers and Their Epileptic Sons

he does believe and he is aware of his own lack of faith ("faith" and "belief" are both English translations of the same Greek root word). The "help" Jesus offers the father is to bolster his faith in the midst of a desperate pessimism induced by years of watching his son suffer. We need not be perfectionists about our faith. This father's faith is mixed, both real and flawed, yet Jesus takes the time to talk to him and does heal his son.

The account of the actual healing occurs in verses 25–27. The story seems to imply that Jesus and the father could have gone on talking because Jesus only rebukes the spirit "when he saw that the crowd was rushing together on them" (v. 25). The language is precise here, "Jesus rebuked the unclean spirit." Jesus can both "heal" the sick and "cast out" demons (see Mark 1:34 and 6:13). Jesus does not heal this boy; he casts out the "unclean spirit" (more of a Jewish phrase that Mark can use synonymously with "demon" as in 7:25 and 29). Jesus addresses the spirit (similar to the father's identification) as "you mute and deaf spirit." Here is another major disconnect that I have with this story. The boy is rolling on the ground in the midst of a seizure and Jesus identifies the spirit by its ability to prevent communication. Jesus expands on the father's identification of a "mute" spirit by adding that it also makes him "deaf." Why not "you seizure inducing spirit"? Our modern medical knowledge tells us that seizures and communication disorders often have the same root cause—irregularities in the brain or neurological function—but ancient societies typically associated epilepsy with supernatural forces. Tuberous Sclerosis induces malformations in brain growth that lead to seizures, autism, communication disorders, emotional imbalances, and an array of related problems. Again, however, Jesus does not speak to this underlying physical condition, but he directly commands the spirit: "Come out of him and never enter him again." While Jesus tells many other demons to "get out of here" (e.g., Mark 1:25 and 5:8), this is the only place in any of the gospels where Jesus gives the additional preventative command "and never enter him again."

Here I must pause to consider the question "Is Pascal demon possessed?" My answer is "no," but then I need to press into the story further to probe the relationship of the spiritual and the physical in my son and the son of the father in this story. The father and Jesus both identify an evil spirit as the cause of the boy's panoply of suffering and danger, but we have already seen that Mark (and other gospel writers as well) can distinguish between spiritual and physical maladies, so we cannot default to the easy answer that "ignorant" ancient persons simply chalked all disease up to evil spirits. However, as noted earlier, the mysterious disorder of epilepsy was almost always attributed to spiritual forces, so there is a bit of cultural bias here that the father accepts and Jesus then probably adopts. I think we have three options here. First, we can claim Jesus' diagnosis can be applied to all epilepsy: all seizures are caused by evil spirits. Second, we can merely attribute this to ancient cultural misunderstanding and view the boy's condition as purely neurological with a culturally conditioned misattribution to an evil spirit. Or third, we can conclude that it is a mixed bag of possibilities that must be decided on a case-by-case basis with the recognition that the ancients tended to spiritualize this condition while we tend to medicalize it. Option three seems to be supported by both Scripture's testimony to the variety of medical and spiritual causes of conditions and our experience of the same mixture. Jesus' unusual additional command that the spirit "never enter him again" perhaps indicates that, while there is an immediate spiritual cause to the boy's inability to communicate (and his seizures!), there may also be a further underlying physical condition. Jesus speaks in Luke 11:24–26 and Matthew 12:43–45 (after the healing of a mute man) of a spirit that is cast out and cannot seem to return because the person it had possessed is balanced and healthy (swept clean and put in order like a house). So, it must gather seven spirits more powerful than itself to be able to take residence again. In the case of this boy, however, Jesus seems to anticipate that the spirit (on its own) will try to return to this boy after being cast out. Perhaps this boy has an underlying medical or neurological condition that makes him particularly susceptible to the invasive and destructive powers of this demon. Jesus' additional prohibition to the spirit indicates that he is acting to further protect the fragile condition of this boy. Pascal is not demon possessed, but he is surely plagued by a physical condition that makes him susceptible to a host of additional threats—spiritual, emotional, physical, and others. It is a reminder that many children like Pascal face a broad range of complex problems and that God responds in many different ways.

## Two Fathers and Their Epileptic Sons

At the command of Jesus, the spirit cries out—the spirit is still the subject of the verbs—and convulses the boy in a particularly violent manner (an adverb is added to the verb for "convulse" here). After this final attack, the spirit departs and the boy appears to be dead, even in the eyes of the crowd. I can only imagine what the father thinks at this moment, and, curiously, he is never mentioned again. Jesus acted suddenly with no warning to the father or anyone else, and the state of events at this point is inconclusive. "Is my son dead? He looks dead. Perhaps this all failed. Perhaps I failed, and now my son is gone forever." I have had these thoughts during some of Pascal's most severe seizures—wondered if I did something wrong or missed something or met circumstances that were simply beyond my power to change. But while the father disappears from the story, the boy appears. Jesus reaches out and takes the hand of the boy, "raises him up," and he stands. That final verb of the story is the only place where the boy is the subject of a verb. He stands with the help of Jesus. Finally, the spirit is gone. His father no longer needs to watch him seize helplessly. Now, with the help of Jesus he can stand. Both of these verbs at the end of this story are also used to describe the resurrection of Jesus. Jesus speaks of "being raised up" after his death (Mark 14:28), and he has told his disciples that after three days he would "arise" (Mark 8:31). Their combination here foreshadows the resurrection, not only of Jesus but also of those who follow him. In these days, I trust in God's help and hold Pascal's hand so that I can lift him up whenever he needs it. However, I long for that day when the resurrection becomes full reality and Pascal can stand on his own and hold my hand.

Jesus' final words to the disciples in verses 28–29 tell us how to live in the meantime. After the conflict and the crowd and the healing, Jesus and the disciples retreat into a home. Once inside, the disciples direct questions about their own inability to Jesus: "Why were we not able to cast it out?" The father and Jesus had dialogued about the issue of ability back in verses 22–23, and the disciples return to that issue here at the closing of the story. Their question reflects my own ongoing questions to God, which reflect my own sense of inability. Why did this have to happen? What can we do for Pascal? Why can't we fix this or that problem? Jesus responds, again redirecting the issue of ability by saying, "This kind [of spirit] is not able to be cast out by anything except prayer." The disciples focused on their ability or lack thereof, but Jesus points them toward God in prayer. In the same way, Jesus redirected the father's question to faith in God ("All things are possible for the one who believes"). One might notice that Jesus never explicitly prays in this story as he does on another occasion when healing a grown man with hearing and speech problems (Mark 7:32–34). This might be an indication of Jesus' constant communion with God, or perhaps an affirmation of the praying faith of the father who begs for help with his lack of faith. In both cases, Jesus instructs the disciples and us on how to make our way through a distressing present before the resurrection while we continue to face our fears and lack of faith and ability. We do it through consistent awareness of a God who is able to give what is needed and through regular, prayerful communion with him. That is the way to healing, now and ultimately.

## Discussion Questions:

1. What do you think about the relationship of demon possession and physical illness? Do you think the New Testament "overdiagnoses" demonic afflictions or that we "underdiagnosis" it? Why?

2. Do you have a particular biblical story that you associate with deeply? What is it? What character do you associate with, and how does it affect the way you read the story?

3. Often, another person's weakness will bring out our own sense of powerlessness. Describe a situation when you felt powerless to help someone. What does this story say about God's presence in the midst of our helplessness?

4. What is the relationship between faith and healing in this story? Have you ever experienced the tension between these two raised by this story? Share a time when you were unsure of your faith in the midst of a crisis or need and how God intervened.

# 7

# My Wife Calls for Welcome

*Speak out for those who cannot speak, for the cause of all those who are ignored.*

—PROVERBS 31:8

FROM THE BEGINNING, MY relationship with my wife, Anne, has been deeply embedded in our discipleship to Christ and our connections to various churches and communities. We had things that brought us together early on (a call to missions and our education), but I have also learned so much about her over the years of our relationship (how she connects to people and how she longs for what is right). God wisely provided connections between our personalities that have helped us bond and grow together and differences that help us balance and challenge one another. We both love people, while Anne is slightly more extroverted and I am slightly more introverted. We enjoy and have done well with our education, though we both tend to lead more with our feelings. We like things clear-cut and make decisions well together. However, Anne is very much externally oriented, ever aware of the world around her (we often joke about her incredible sense of smell), while I have all the intuition of the family and thrive much more in an internal world (we also often joke about my convoluted daydreams). I come to write this chapter with great trepidation because I know that Anne will read it and give me her honest critique of it. Yet, I tremble even more so because this chapter requires me to step into the soul of another person, a person whom I love dearly and respect profoundly, and then describe her experience of following Christ with Pascal from the inside out. Because I sense that I know her so well, I feel an even greater responsibility to get this chapter "right"—to capture what she feels and why she acts. With the Spirit's help, I pray that I can give you a small window into her, her love for Pascal, and her passion for God's justice.

For your sake and for mine, I need to depict how Anne has responded to and processed our experiences with Pascal very differently than I did. This will help me express her call for welcome and help you understand how that is integral to her particular reflection of the image of God. Perhaps because she carried Pascal for nine months in her womb she struggled more with accusing doubts about unwittingly contributing to Pascal's disorder. "What if I did something wrong while I was pregnant? Could I have avoided anything that might have prevented this from happening?" While it is true that we cried together often in the months after Pascal's diagnosis, I believe our tears emerged from somewhat different emotional urges. I am bent toward grief and a sense of loss. Anne was overwhelmed with the situation, stunned by the shock and weight of it all at once. My emotions tend to swirl deep inside while my exterior is unruffled. Anne's emotions press forth through her face, in her voice, and very much on her shirt sleeve. If my sinful tendency was toward despair and depression, her sinful tendency was toward anger and impatience. I have and can become pessimistic about Pascal's situation and future, while Anne reroutes his difficulties into calls for action. These differences often come to a head when we are dealing with doctors and teachers. When we don't feel Pascal is getting the right treatment or the best care I take the long and slow approach, waiting to see what happens and selectively inserting our perspective. Anne, on the other hand, often speaks of her "mama bear" reactions. She senses something is wrong and starts to push back instinctively. When she sees the thing that is not right she will speak to it directly and ask for things to be done differently.

I hope in light of this introduction you will not be surprised when I say my wife is a prophet. She doesn't like it when I call her

## My Wife Calls for Welcome

that, but I have been convinced for years (and I think I have won her over) that prophecy is her predominant spiritual gift (Rom 12:6, 1 Cor 12:10). She falls in a tradition of other female prophets in Scripture such as Huldah in 2 Kings 22 or Anna, one of Anne's namesakes, in Luke 2. Identifying Anne as a prophetess compels me to offer a bit of clarification on two biblical concepts: prophecy and righteousness. Prophecy is often popularly portrayed as prediction—prophets speak on behalf of God about events in the future. If we look at what the prophets of the Old Testament (and the New as well) actually do though, we see something else. The prophets (Elijah, Isaiah, Amos, etc.) address the vast majority of their speech to the present circumstances of their audience. A minority of their words from God are about future events, but when they are these events are often right around the corner. Only a sliver of their sayings are about the distant future. Recalling Soren (he is a prophet and a son of a prophetess, an ironic turn on Amos 7:14), let us take a look at how this works out in Jeremiah. Jeremiah chapters 2–3 is God's summons to the people of Jerusalem and Judah to repent. After this in 4:5–31, Jeremiah vividly and emotionally envisions the fall of Jerusalem, an event coming in the near future. Likewise, Jeremiah 7:1—10:16 focuses on the disobedience of God's people, while 10:17–25 depicts the soon-coming exile. One of the few places where God opens a window for Jeremiah into the distant future is in 31:31–34. Here Jeremiah speaks of a dramatically new covenant between God and God's people, a passage cited and applied in Hebrews 8. Most of the time God calls prophets to speak to God's people and their leaders and to speak against their unjust and disobedient actions (see the sections of Jeremiah above and Amos chs. 1–2). Thus, Anne embodies her calling as a prophet when she speaks to people here and now and speaks about injustice from God's perspective.

The second biblical concept is righteousness. The Hebrew *tsedekah* and the Greek *dikaiosunē* can both be translated into English as either justice or righteousness, or in their adjective forms as either just or righteous. Thus, while we may separate out legal or forensic nuances for "justice" and moral or spiritual nuances for "righteousness," the biblical authors did not share this same distinction in the same way. For them, these nuances belonged in one word group. A prophet speaks out against injustice/unrighteousness and calls the

Holding Hands with Pascal

people back to God's just/righteous ways. This justice/righteousness is first and foremost a characteristic of God: "I am the Lord; I act with steadfast love, justice, and righteousness in the earth (Jer 9:24; see also Ps 11:7, Matt 6:33, Rom 1:17). God's justice/righteousness does issue forth in holy judgment of what is wrong: "God is a righteous judge, and a God who has indignation every day" (Ps 7:11; see also 2 Thess 1:5, Acts 17:31, Rom 1:18). Even more though, Scripture asserts that God's righteousness/justice prompts God to save and redeem people: "God put forward Jesus as a sacrifice of atonement by his blood, effective through faith. He did this to show his righteousness . . . to prove at the present time that he himself is righteous and that he justifies the one who has faith in Jesus (Rom 3:25–26; see also Ps 31:1, Is 45:8, Mic 7:9). Righteousness/justice is not only a characteristic of God, for God expects people to live this out particularly through the care of those who are vulnerable and in need: "Speak out, judge righteously, defend the rights of the poor and needy" (Prov 31:9; see also Ps 72:2, Amos 5:24, 1 John 3:10). The call of the prophets of the Old Testament connects to justice/righteousness in all directions. God is righteous and so will judge people justly when they do not carry out righteousness and justice on earth as God has commanded. Anne's concern for God's justice/righteousness takes on this same dynamic. She feels God's righteous anger against injustice and longs to see justice and righteousness done in society, especially for the sake of those who are most at risk.

What then does it mean to carry out God's justice/righteousness for children with special needs or adults who are differently-abled in our time and place? In *Theology and Down Syndrome* Amos Yong writes, "Justification is not only God's pronouncement of justice but also God's liberation from injustice. . . . [This] benefits all, judges and redeems the fallen powers, and enables the renewal of a just world."[1] Yong notes three effects of this justice/righteousness: it is good for all people, it identifies and begins to change unjust political and economic "powers," and it helps societies carry out the good and just things God desires. What does such a society look like? Yong also says, "From a disability perspective, God declares God's acceptance of our lives through the welcome and embrace of others."[2] That is,

---

1. Yong, *Theology and Down Syndrome*, 255–56.
2. Yong, *Theology and Down Syndrome*, 252.

## My Wife Calls for Welcome

as those empowered to carry out God's righteousness through the Spirit, we tangibly express the reality of God's justice/righteousness when we wholeheartedly welcome others, especially those who are vulnerable and excluded.[3] I believe that "welcome" goes beyond mere "inclusion," for it connotes a quality of warmth, joy, and relationship that is more than just being allowed in. Thus, we have the title of this chapter: my wife calls for welcome. As a prophet led by God's Spirit, Anne calls families, churches, and institutions to welcome Pascal and others in similarly challenging and vulnerable conditions.

Home and family is the place where welcome is most natural. God designed homes and families to be welcoming, and many cultures have strong expectations that you care for your family members and treat guests kindly. Homes can be broken and harmful places, but if that tragedy occurs, it is often because a family has failed to welcome its own members. Welcome can be a natural and normal response, but people with special needs present special challenges. What do you do when your guest can't eat 90 percent of the food you are serving, or when basic household features (such as stairs or screen doors) may be harmful or misused? Pascal was on a special diet for a few years and could have almost no carbohydrates (no bread, pasta, chips, etc.)—staple fare for most children his age. He was very unsteady on stairs even at six, and he was big enough, clumsy enough, and unaware enough to fall down stairs or push right through screen doors. The children of families who did welcome us into their homes often did not know how to play with Pascal. Sometimes they avoided him or were obviously (and understandably) frustrated by his loud and demanding manner. How do we welcome in these situations? What did my wife call for?

We find this summons in Isaiah 58:6–7: "Is not this the fast that I [God] choose: to loose the bonds of injustice, to undo the thongs of the yoke, to let the oppressed go free, and to break every yoke? Is it not to share your bread with the hungry, and bring the homeless poor into your house, when you see the naked, to cover them, and not to hide yourself from your own kin?" These two verses call for freedom and personal involvement: to let the oppressed go free and to bring the homeless into your house. While welcome typically applies to

---

3. Reynolds, *Vulnerable Communion*, 239–45.

a specific place with boundaries, it generates freedom within those boundaries. So my wife sought for Pascal to have the freedom to play, eat, and rest within the homes that we visited. Anne called for this welcome many times, seeking out people who would share our journey with Pascal. Only a few responded. The small numbers still grieve us at moments, but those who did welcome us have made all the difference. We have seen genuine welcome from a few brothers and sisters in Christ who treated us like family. Our friends regularly asked what Pascal could and could not eat, planning ahead to accommodate his dietary needs. Some good friends with a pool regularly opened their home to us, knowing Pascal loved to swim. They didn't mind when Pascal made a mess by pulling off book after book of their *Animal Babies* series to look at each one. They made their own homes as free and as open as our own home—a good definition of welcome.

Our friends seemed to be almost as sensitive as Anne about how their own children treated Pascal. This is a case where welcome needs to be trained even in a home and with a family. Pascal can be very difficult to relate to and deal with, and even I have my own struggles coping with Pascal's behavior. He acts impulsively to take toys he wants. He is both big and very immature for his age, so when he gets excited he can also get overly physical. When he doesn't get what he wants, he can throw very loud tantrums. All of this can be disconcerting and even frightening to other children. Our home has a second story with a play room and an extra bedroom. We hosted several gatherings of our Followers & Friends Sunday school class in our home. On a few occasions, the kids (including Soren) would lock Pascal out of the upstairs because they didn't want him to disrupt their games. Anne would notice Pascal crying quickly, but so would the other parents. They were just as concerned as we were about the situation and would help us resolve it. I would calm Pascal down, and they would explain to the kids that it is not right to shut Pascal out. These parents got personally involved to help educate and train their own children on how to respond to Pascal. These kids (Ian, Bradley, Madeleine, Ashlyn, and Eliana) became some of Pascal's favorite friends. They were still kids, and problems still flared up, but they all learned how to play together with ease and joy—another good definition of welcome.

## My Wife Calls for Welcome

The church is another place where everyone should find a welcome as the body of Christ expresses the grace of God to the world. While we found welcome in some smaller Christian gatherings in homes, church services presented new problems. As I mentioned, most of the Old Testament prophets were sent by God to confront God's people, and particularly the leaders of God's people, with their unrighteous actions and choices. Needless, to say this created an uneasy relationship. For instance, Isaiah told King Hezekiah that he would recover from a seemingly fatal illness, but right on the heels of this announcement he condemns Hezekiah, prophesying the destruction and exile of Judah (see both in 2 Kings 20). James has to prophetically confront the churches he writes to because they habitually exclude and shame the poor (James 2:1–7). And so Anne has had a somewhat rocky relationship with churches we have attended and with the church as a whole. She is deeply connected to them relationally and spiritually but simultaneously (and perhaps causally) aware of the subtle and persistent wrongs that infect churches. To make matters worse, by making them more complicated, church-going people often have good intentions. Injustice toward the vulnerable and different is often fueled by ignorance, assumptions, and structures rather than by ill will. Let me illustrate with a few examples that make us sometimes smile and sometimes cringe in hindsight.

We learned early on that we could not simply visit a church as most churches are not prepared to welcome and provide the extra care needed for children with special needs. You can't just drop off a toddler who occasionally has fully generalized seizures into a typical church's children's ministry. Our eight-year-old Pascal is about as big as most ten-year-olds, but he functions at the level of a three-year-old. So what Sunday school class does he go to? Certainly he can't sit through a (very adult-oriented) service with us, so what do we do? Anne's response was frustration with the injustice that emerges out of a lack of foresight, out of an assumption that all children are "normal." If you are not "normal," then we don't have a natural slot for you to fit into, and if you have no slot to fit into, then you are not welcomed. The best thing Anne could do here was to initiate awkward conversations about how a church already strapped for volunteers and resources could accommodate Pascal in ways that would welcome all of us. Anne was also keenly aware when people at church looked askance at us when Pascal had a tantrum or behaved in other ways that seemed inappropriate for a child of his physical age. To have this happen at church, where we should be welcomed, made it cut all the more deeply. Unlike Down Syndrome or some other disorders, Pascal has no physical characteristics to mark his differentness and difficulties. We sometimes joke about getting him a t-shirt that reads, "I had part of my brain removed. What's your excuse for misbehaving?" Anne's prophetic response to these situations was often through actions later complemented by words (see the many symbolic actions performed by Ezekiel and Jeremiah). We simply carried on. We lived life in all of our unusualness and exceptionality with God's help in the midst of the community, thereby testifying to the welcome of God that had not quite yet come to expression in the church. We also took any opportunities God presented to tell people about Pascal and to introduce them to him (he would often talk about his shirt or a stuffed animal or where we were going for lunch that day). We believe these personal encounters with Pascal, over time, can turn the tide from misunderstanding to compassion within Christ's body.

Many of us know that Jesus tells us, "Whoever welcomes one such child in my name welcomes me" (Matt 18:5). Yet, we also know of many times when someone has put "a stumbling block before one of these little ones who believe in me" (Matt 18:6). On one painful occasion we tried visiting a Wednesday evening service at a church we had attended for some time. We checked in with the staff, gave what we thought was some appropriate advice, and then left Soren and Pascal there as we went off to an adult class. Later when we picked Pascal up, the young and well-meaning children's pastor informed us that Pascal had been disruptive, not sitting still, and trying to leave on several occasions. He just didn't behave and didn't fit well. Anne was incensed and as we left said to me, "Of course he didn't! What did they expect! We are never coming back on Wednesday night again. I'm ready to leave this church." The lack of welcome (again as unintentional as it was) left us with a burning sense of exclusion from this gathering of God's people. Soon after, we did leave that church, and in our search for a new church we learned something about what it means to be welcomed. We contacted the children's pastor at a different church that we wanted to visit and explained Pascal's circumstances. She responded and said that they did not have any children with special needs in the church and she didn't know exactly what to do, but she wanted to talk to us and figure out what we needed. Welcome is not necessarily having it all figured out ahead of time, but about being compassionately responsive when someone who does not fit your expectations and needs things you are unused to giving. Anne's prophetic voice was welcomed, which made a way for Pascal to be welcomed. She spoke up for Pascal's needs, and we did find a way for Pascal to have a place of freedom and relationships. Even though he was eight, he joined the pre-kindergarten class and fit right in with the help of a devoted and caring helper, Miss Peggy. After a while he slid right into the routine of the class, and we were often told that he was one of the best-behaved kids that morning. The children's ministry staff made it possible for Pascal to join the (rather boisterous) children's worship service where Soren and others could welcome him and help him participate. Recently, he transitioned to the kindergarten class along with Miss Peggy, and he is doing great. That welcome has paid off in long-term benefits. The freedom and personal involvement offered to Pascal made this church what all churches should be—a place of welcome where Pascal is free to worship and play and has loving relationship with other children and adults. Our whole family now feels at home in this congregation, and we search for ways to welcome other "little ones" as well.

A few homes heard the call to welcome, and the church has responded too, but Anne has had the most—and most heated—confrontations with school systems and insurance companies. This makes perfect sense because the prophets throughout Scripture are called to confront the very leaders and institutions set up to promote the well-being of God's people, indeed of all people. Institutions like this face three particular challenges when it comes to welcoming people who are different and vulnerable. First, similar to home and church, we believe schools and medical organizations have a distinct role in welcoming people with special challenges and needs. They bear a burden of responsibility. Second, institutions tend to be larger organizations and can become hardened into procedures and policies. Policies and procedures become impersonal and tend to route people into categories, which can limit or frustrate the welcome offered to those who are different. Third, power and normativity come into play in institutions. Power can blind or at least shield us from weakness and difference and thus defray our ability to respond with welcome and compassion. Institutions thrive on stability and predictability, so difference is an anomaly to be dealt with and assimilated rather than an opportunity for welcome and change. Let me say clearly and gratefully that we have worked with a number of very kind, intelligent, and compassionate teachers, doctors, and administrators over the years. Yet, institutions still have these tendencies; injustice seems to grow in the cracks of bylaws and handbooks and surreptitiously creeps into practices and actions carried out by (sometimes unwitting) agents of those institutions. This has prompted Anne to call for welcome on many occasions.

Scripture gives some special attention to welcoming those who have special needs in the larger and more public domains of society. In the midst of various ordinances dealing with stealing, fraud, and slander, Leviticus 19:14 says, "You shall not revile the deaf or put a stumbling block before the blind; you shall fear your God: I am the LORD." This piece of the Old Testament law prohibits public shaming of those who cannot hear and answer (the deaf) and warns the people to remove those obstacles the blind may not see. In both cases, special responses are required to make sure these two sets of people with unusual needs are welcome in public. Amos 5:12 accuses the unrighteous leaders of Israel of "pushing aside the needy at the gate" (see also 2:7). The city gate was the place of public discourse and business dealings (see 5:10-11 on this). The powerful and wealthy have the capacity to simply not give a place to those who are weaker and in need; however, God sees and condemns such actions. Proverbs 31 (cited at the opening of this chapter) warns the king to not forget and pervert the rights of the afflicted (v. 5). The king is responsible for speaking out for those who are ignored, for judging righteously, and for defending the rights of the needy (vv. 8-9). God calls for the needy and the unusually afflicted to be welcomed in the power-brokering spaces of society so that they may have a safe place and a heard voice.

One of the challenges we face regarding welcome is over the issue of labels. Most technically and specifically, Pascal has a genetic disorder identified as Tuberous Sclerosis Complex, but it is far from simple, for that disorder has disordered a number of other parts of his health and development. At first, we resisted the label of autism for Pascal. He had some of the clinical elements (speech delay, underdeveloped social skills) but not others (repetitive habits, no eye contact). Anne distinctly did not want the label of autism to become a badge that would bar Pascal from welcome in school, work, or other places. Over time though, we discovered that some key therapy services (Applied Behavior Analysis, or ABA for short) were being denied to Pascal by our insurance company because he lacked this label. We learned that labels and welcome have a lot to do with one another. The labels we apply to people and the labels they adopt impact how and how much we welcome them. Anne talked to Pascal's doctors and consulted with our nearby therapy center. I negotiated most of the insurance complexities. We eventually discovered that Pascal could fit under the label of Pervasive Developmental Disorder (PDD), which qualified him for ABA therapy. This was a lot of time and work for the opening of one door to one therapy service, but it was worth it for we believe his ABA therapy has been a key element in Pascal's tremendous development over the past few years. Labels can be avenues or roadblocks to welcome. We can use them, but we should use them without a rigid grip and always in the interest of loving welcome.

 Pascal went through our local school's preschool program for children with special needs. When he turned five, it was time to transition him into an elementary school. This presented a host of options and new mazes to navigate, and Anne had to call for welcome on many occasions. It began with the realization that the elementary-aged children with special needs in our school district were funneled to one particular school with designated Life Skills classrooms. School system lingo uses the language of the "least restrictive environment" to talk about welcome. The school tries to find the environment that will place the fewest restrictions or limitations on the development of a child. It is a good aim, but one complicated by institutional dynamics. The most welcoming and least restrictive environment, in our opinion, was a regular kindergarten classroom. Accommodations would have to be made, but we had seen Pascal fit into other "normal" situations with children his age and believed this to be best, rather than being placed into a "sheltered" classroom largely separate from other children. We had many meetings with school officials who thought the Life Skills class would be best for him. We visited those classes and were unconvinced. Anne resisted Pascal being forced down one predictable track that we believed would limit his opportunities and development—essentially putting a stumbling block in front of him. We did get him into a regular kindergarten in the same school building as Soren, but unforeseen stumbling blocks appeared all around. Pascal had very different needs than another boy who had autism at this school. The aide assigned to them had difficulties handling them both. Pascal would sometimes wander away if bored or run away if upset, and the school and teachers were not equipped to deal with this kind of security issue. The regular kindergarten teacher was overwhelmed with twenty-four other children in the classroom and could not accommodate the amount of difference Pascal introduced into such a large group. Could she get all the scissors out and put them away each time they were used just because Pascal would use them inappropriately at the wrong times? No, this, along with a myriad of other little things, was just too much to handle. We came to realize the welcome Anne called for and that Pascal received was not going to work. The very real demands and limitations faced by the school made it impossible for Pascal to find welcome there.

After further negotiating, we moved Pascal over to the Life Skills class. More awkward transitions came and new routines had to be learned, but in a few months Pascal was doing well. We still urge the school to do all that they can for him, giving him the best opportunities to grow and learn in as many ways possible. What we did not expect is that God would use this shift to allow us to welcome others. By moving into a class dedicated to children with special needs we came into contact with other children and families facing similar challenges. That has opened up opportunities for us to come to know and welcome others. When Pascal turned eight Anne had the great idea to throw a party for him and his classmates at a local bowling alley. The children knew the bowling alley from some recent field trips, and when we mentioned it to Pascal he just about burst with excitement. He asked every day for the next two weeks about his party. The day came and five other kids from Pascal's class came—most with their parents but one child was generously brought by Pascal's teacher. The kids loved every minute of it: throwing the

*My Wife Calls for Welcome*

ball down the alley, cheering for their friends, opening presents, eating cupcakes. We had a blast (and a few dropped bowling balls that made us nervous). Near the end of the party, one mom commented that her little boy had never been invited to a birthday party before. It hit us that the call for welcome must be heard by us as well. Anne will continue to call for welcome for Pascal, and we have heard the call from God to welcome others into our lives in ways that offer the combination of sensitive freedom and loving relationships that God calls right and just.

## Discussion Questions:

1. Describe the perspective of righteousness/justice described in this chapter. Pick one of the Old Testament prophets and find a place where they call out for righteousness and justice.

2. Have you seen any prophets in your life, or have you felt like one yourself? Tell about a time when you or someone you know confronted injustice on behalf of someone with special needs. How did it turn out?

3. What are the places you find the least welcoming? The most welcoming? How is God present in these places? If you work in a large organization or institution what can you do to make it more welcoming to those who do not "naturally" fit in?

4. How do you welcome people? How can you personally expand your ability to welcome others, especially those who are vulnerable and ignored—those whom God tells us to make sure we welcome?

# 8

# A Father's Failures

*Do not be overcome by evil, but overcome evil with good.*
—ROMANS 12:21

AND NOW WE COME to a chapter about me. As I have admitted repeatedly, I am recounting all these stories and reflections about Pascal from my own perspective, so a chapter on myself may seem redundant, but it plays a key role in the transition to the second half of this book. I recognize that I have been in control of the contents of this book, and control can be dangerous and illusory. I may have subtly convinced you (and myself) that I have it all figured out, that I am a fantastic father, that I am a strong person. I hope to disabuse you and myself of that notion in the writing of this chapter. The theme of weakness mentioned in the previous chapters will become a guiding focus in the following chapters. Following Christ with Pascal has taught me that weakness is at the center of Jesus' ministry and message, at the core of the corporate body of Christ, and at the heart of our discipleship. The weakness we hide gestates fear and anger that separate us from each other and from God. The weakness we share can blossom forth in trust and love that bind us to God and to each other. This chapter is my meager attempt to share my weakness, my failures with you before God in the hope that we can all come to know God and one another better in Christ.

I have written of our shock and grief as we came to terms with Pascal's condition and of how Anne and I responded differently. Crying was good for me because it helped me share in an experience of grief, especially with Anne but also with others. In the moments when I hurt beyond crying, I slipped into despair. I didn't want to slog through this mire of being a parent or a husband or a disciple. I wanted to quit, to give up, to relinquish any and all responsibility, because some instinct in me said that this was the only way to escape the fatigue and fear that I felt. Kierkegaard (our Soren's namesake) said this about despair: "Will you in doubleness of mind despair, because all is lost (yes, so you think) yet with the Eternal all is to be won! Will you in doubleness of mind despair? Have you considered what it is to despair? Alas, it is to deny that God is love! Think that over properly, one who despairs abandons himself (yes, so you think); nay, he abandons God!"[1] In overreaction and smallsightedness I could think that all was lost. It did feel like the only way out was to abandon myself—the only life I knew, but it was really me abandoning the God who declares, "I am the Lord, merciful and gracious, slow to anger, and abounding in steadfast love" (Ex 34:6). I forgot the love God revealed and demonstrated to us in the weakness and sacrifice of Jesus (1 John 4:9–10). Despair takes our current painful situation as the only possibility, forgetting the infinite possibilities of our infinite God, and I faced several calm and terrifying moments contemplating despair as the end of my journey with Pascal.

One of the manifestations of despair that plagues me most is to simply do nothing. If I cannot lift my eyes beyond the horizon of my capabilities to see God's provision, then why bother to make any effort? If we have failed to make good friends because it is too difficult to navigate the complexities of Pascal's needs, then why try to meet new people? If the insurance company tells us that they will not cover this or that type of therapy, then why go through the effort of filing an appeal if it will just be denied? Doing nothing can be a powerful testimony to a God who works intricately and ultimately on our behalf, but mine was borne of a sense of hopelessness and

---

1. Kierkegaard, *Purity of Heart*, 151.

exhaustion. Sometimes I do not pursue medical leads that might help Pascal. Sometimes I don't press for fuller services from our school system. Sometimes I let him get away with bad behavior because I am tired of dealing with it. In times like this, Anne's tireless hunger and thirst for righteousness is the summons I need to continue to walk with and advocate for Pascal. She calls me to speak out and defend the rights of the needy (Prov 31:9). She transfers God's grace to me in ways that bring me out of my despair and inaction. She is a companion and a gift to me.

Despair can be a natural (and perhaps necessary) stop along a longer journey toward new openness to life, others, and God. Jean Vanier, an advocate for and caring friend of those facing severe challenges and disabilities, captured this well:

> Many times parents of people with disabilities have told me about the shock they received at the birth of their child. Then they discovered that their child was leading them from a world of power and competition into a world of tenderness and compassion. Crises and unexpected changes can lead us to denial, despair, anger, and revolt, but these feelings can gradually help us to accept reality as it is and discover in the new situation new energies, a new freedom, and a new meaning of life and of the world.[2]

We felt that shock, that grief, that despair. Note, though, that Vanier states that these feelings "gradually help" us to find new meaning and purpose. These feelings we dread so much are part of God's gift to us to move us forward, for weakness creates an awareness of our need for God, a God who lives with us in a way that neither eradicates weakness nor ends in despair. This is why the "poor in spirit" are blessed (Matt 5:3)—they recognize their poverty and need and open themselves to God's provision. This combination of life and weakness is enshrined in the life of Jesus. God's Christ is both crucified and resurrected. Resurrection does not undo crucifixion, does not erase it as something that never happened. Jesus lives a new and miraculous life that still includes the wounds of the cross. Revelation gives us the picture of a slaughtered lamb that conquers (5:5–6). Jesus does not stop being a slaughtered lamb when he conquers evil; he is

---

2. Vanier, *Becoming Human*, 128.

## A Father's Failures

always both lamb and conqueror, weak and victorious. While I occasionally return to that moment in my journey and face despair again, this book is a testimony to the larger story of God's living presence before, in, and beyond my despair.

I may have passed largely out of the stage of potential despair over the years, but two other persistent and subtle failings have taken its place: frustration and fantasy. Both of these are driven by an infectious belief in my (deeply Americanized) soul that God put all us on this earth to accomplish things as the highest expression of our created existence. I, and most of you reading this book, drink the cultural water that tells us our bodies and lives must be able, efficient, and productive. We are only valuable insofar as we "exhibit qualities and perform in ways that are useful and thus generate capital."[3] Many pernicious lies have some connection to truth, and in this case God did command Adam and Eve to "be fruitful and multiply" (Gen 1:28) and directed Adam to tend the garden of Eden (Gen 2:15). To work and produce is not the total purpose for our existence, nor should we allow our Americanized (and not necessarily Christian) standards determine what counts as healthy human productivity. All too often, however, I slip back into this very familiar perspective, prioritizing productivity as the measure of my life and of Pascal's life. This leads me to be frustrated when Pascal falls short of my expectations and to fantasize about a life free from Pascal's limitations.

I admit that I experience aggravating frustration with Pascal. Sometimes we work on the same task or activity over and over and over, and he does not get it. Potty training was a long, slow, and messy process; he still puts his shirts on backwards. Even more infuriating are Pascal's behavioral problems. He can be dangerously impulsive, walking out of the house without warning if he gets it in his mind that he wants to play outside. He will throw, jump on, and break things in the house even though we have tried to train him out of such behaviors. Sometimes he will ask for the same activity or item incessantly ("Gum? Gum? Gum, please? I want gum? Gum, please?") until I want earplugs to block him out. He can throw loud, disruptive, and long tantrums over the tiniest things. He will scream, cry, and flail until snot is pouring out of his nose and I can barely restrain him. At times like this I

---

3. Reynolds, *Vunerable Communion*, 90.

ache to make the screaming stop. I have screamed back at him to try to shock him out of a tantrum. I have been tempted to smack Pascal just to put an end to the noise and chaos, which often spreads to our other kids, compounding the problem. Sometimes Pascal simply refuses to listen to me and will try to run away. I will resort to grabbing his hair when I am desperate and don't know how else to control him. I know the concoction of anger, exhaustion, and exasperation that leads me to contemplate and enact this kind of violence. It frightens me, and I know it is profoundly wrong.

People often comment on how patient and caring I am. I know God helps me walk with Pascal in love and compassion, but I also am deeply aware of these failures. I thank God I have never hit Pascal, but I regret all those moments of shouting and hair-pulling. I see something else inside myself, something that Jean Vanier has felt and captured in self-revealing words:

> I have experienced my own limits at certain moments, times when I realized there was great anger and violence rising up in me with respect to certain people with disabilities. Maybe it was because they seemed to be provoking me; maybe their anguish and feelings of loneliness called for my full attention at a time when I was not able to give it; maybe it was because I failed to alleviate their screams and their anguish. Or maybe it was deeper than all that: perhaps the anguish of those with intellectual disabilities awoke my own anguish.[4]

I have especially felt these failures and rising tides of anger when I am pressed beyond my capacity or simply at a loss about what I can do. Sometimes Pascal asks too much of me and I respond out of impatience and anger. But I know love and trust are built upon tenderness, gentleness, and patience. As I am filled with the Holy Spirit, I know I can show these to Pascal and engender loving and trusting responses from him, yet I am simultaneously repulsed by my own poverty—my lack of patience, the ease of overreacting, the ugliness of my own anger. In this mix, I experience a small taste of the blessedness of the poor in spirit because I get to participate in God's kingdom when kindness flows through me to Pascal.

4. Vanier, *Becoming Human*, 100.

## A Father's Failures

I also admit I sometimes fantasize about a "good and productive" life without Pascal. Pascal's disordered genes, medical requirements, and developmental limitations all fly in the face of the American "gospel" of effectiveness and productivity. Pascal's unusual and sometimes intense needs are hobbling shackles on productivity—his, our family's, and mine. I occasionally struggle to identify the significance of Pascal's life. I want him to be healthy. I want him to have all the therapy he can get and develop as much as he can. But what if he lives most of his life depending on others because of his demanding medical needs? Wouldn't he be a drain on us, on our society? I try to push that thought away because it forces me either to give up on him or to invasively reevaluate my own beliefs about the value of human life before God. I have at times contemplated what our life could be without Pascal. What if he had never been born or had been born "normal"? Think of all the things we could do, all the books I could write, all the ministries we could lead! When Pascal was in the pediatric ICU hooked up to a variety of wires in a post-seizure coma-like state, I daydreamed of the freedom we could have if he had died. He wouldn't need thousands of dollars of medical care. We would not have our lives dramatically interrupted by repeated hospital stays. I can only shamefully reflect on this as a very sick hope driven by the consuming obsession that our only purpose is to do things for God in the world and to be productive members of society. I fail both God and Pascal when I allow this destructive perspective to define Pascal's life, to define our life together.

God declares all creation is "very good" (Gen 1:31) before Adam and Eve have any chance to be fruitful. God also declares "it is not good for the man to be alone" (Gen 2:18), indicating that relationship is foundational to the goodness of human life in God's eyes. When I actually express my fantasy of freedom from Pascal, it tells him I do not want him in this world, that he is no good to me or to God. If I see Pascal as a terrible disappointment, then he will sink into despair; but if I tell Pascal that I am glad, delighted that he exists, then he can blossom as a person made in God's image.[5] God has created us to need these mutual affirmations, and as God has corrected and enabled us, our family has done this for Pascal and each other. I can see Pascal's joy. He enjoys his life.

5. Hauerwas and Vanier, *Living Gently*, 69.

## Holding Hands with Pascal

Pascal spent several days in the hospital recovering from his brain surgery. That was a long and difficult haul for his body and spirit, but near the end of his stay we were able to take him out for a brief visit to a nearby playground. The left side of his face was very swollen from the fluid that was still draining after the surgery, and he wore a little red fisherman's cap to protect his shaved and scarred head from the summer sun. But despite all that he had been through and his continuing weakness, he was delighted with his few minutes of outside play that afternoon. He smiled a quirky, crooked smile as he bumbled after his brother around the jungle gym. Now, a few years later, Pascal looks forward to almost every day of school, anticipating his daily "specials" (art class, music class, gym, etc.) and seeing his friends. At home, Pascal loves it when we wrestle or when I tickle him. He just can't get enough. He runs through the house with his little sister, having a ball. Jean Vanier identifies this kind of joyful celebration as one of the key constituents of community. Again, he captures our life well in simple words:

> By celebrating, I mean to laugh, to fool around, to have fun, to give thanks together for life. When we are laughing together with belly laughs we are all the same. We're all just belly laughing. Some of our people are really crazy and really funny. They are funny because they are crazy, and they are crazy because they are funny. It's super to be with them.[6]

Pascal is definitely crazy and funny and super. When we affirm that being with Pascal is good, we free him both to have joy and to share joy. We celebrate and laugh and play together. It is no accident that Revelation describes God's grand renewal of the universe as a big party—the "marriage banquet of the Lamb" (19:9 and 21:9). To be with God in this final and fullest way is to celebrate with joy, a joy that seems improbable throughout most of Revelation with its repeated calls to endure in the midst of horrific events (e.g., 13:9–10; 14:12–13). Pascal's joyful life with us reflects the ultimate celebration of the reunion of God and God's people even as we endure the failures and difficulties of our distressing present.

---

6. Hauerwas and Vanier, *Living Gently*, 37.

## A Father's Failures

This is a small sample of my failures—the ones I struggle with the most and that I hope offer some solace to others who struggle. I have come to see weakness as a gift from God. It can drive us apart when we hide our failures and vulnerabilities in shame and fear, but when we open up our weaknesses we find God is present and we are drawn together. As I have contemplated my own failures repeatedly while writing this chapter I have found consolation in two key ways. The first is the merciful and forgiving nature of our God. I quoted the beginning of the classic statement of God's character from Exodus 34 above: "The Lord, a God merciful and gracious, slow to anger, and abounding in steadfast love and faithfulness" (v. 6). The next verse goes on to say God keeps "steadfast love for the thousandth generation, forgiving iniquity and transgression and sin" (v. 7). God does judge the guilty, but while God's love and forgiveness last a thousand generations, God's judgment only lasts three or four generations (see the end of v. 7). I know that God is set against my sins and failures, but I know that mercy triumphs over judgment (James 2:13). I can share my weaknesses and failures in this chapter because I have come to know the love and forgiveness in Christ that drives out fear (1 John 4:18). I do not have to fear God because I have seen God's love for me demonstrated in the life, weakness, and death of Christ. Receiving God's love enables and summons each one of us to love one another (1 John 4:7) even in the midst of our weakness and failures.

My second point of consolation recalls the opening verse for this chapter: do not be overcome by evil, but overcome evil with good (Rom 12:21). This verse reminds us that being overcome by evil is a real possibility in the Christian life. My failures are not some kind of awful aberration far outside the normal experience of God's people and of parents trying to follow Christ with a special needs child. They are, instead, part of the struggle I should expect on the path to freedom from failure and freedom to love and serve others. But even more, this verse reminds me that evil can be overcome with good. Built into every exhortation in Paul's letters is the assertion that grace is available to make obedience possible. In Christ and through the Spirit, I can overcome evil with good. I have seen this at work in very practical ways. As with the epileptic boy of Mark 9, I think Pascal's physical and mental disabilities render him susceptible to evil in unusual ways. This has tempted me to overcome the evils that plague

Pascal with other (greater?) evils, but I now see that I cannot do that, for it is ultimately destructive. As my frustration rises Pascal's frustration rises. If Pascal attempts to run away from me and I grab his hair, then I teach him to fear me and to grab other people's hair. I have seen it happen. He runs away even more quickly and he can be harsh with other children. When I respond with gentleness and kindness, Pascal learns to trust me, to listen to me, and I have seen the change in Pascal's behavior based on my behavior. When met with my love for him, his tantrums lose their energy like a hurricane that has just run onto unmovable land. That hurricane carries destructive forces when it hits land, but then its power fades as it runs aground and settles into a manageable rain. Overcoming evil with good is a slow path that requires God-given help, but as my failures and impatience decrease I see good surge over the evils of impulsivity, frustration, and disobedience in Pascal.

I pray for two results from this chapter. First, may this confession of my failures, made possible by my confidence in God's love and mercy, inspire you to abandon despair and shame and allow God's love to flow into and through your weaknesses. Second, may we all become conduits of God's love in our weakness and overcome evil through the goodness and gentleness supplied by the Spirit.

## Discussion Questions:

1. What losses or challenges in your life have brought out your deepest weaknesses and greatest failures? How did your respond to those failures?
2. What weaknesses and failures are you prone to experience: despair, anger, passivity, overreaction, or others?
3. What attributes of God offer you the most hope and consolation? Which Scriptures do you turn to in your darkest times?
4. How have you seen good overcome evil in your own life? Where do you currently need this to happen?

# 9

# Holding Hands with Pascal

*... and a little child shall lead them.*
—ISAIAH 11:6

OVER THE YEARS WE have made many visits to the Cincinnati Children's Hospital. This wonderful hospital houses one of the top Tuberous Sclerosis clinics in America, offering multifaceted care from a team of doctors and other professionals to children facing the many complexities of this disorder. Whenever it is possible the whole family goes to Cincinnati (about a three-hour drive from our home) for Pascal's checkups. We try to make it a fun family trip with a stop at the Children's Museum and our favorite ice cream parlor. Though sometimes this is not possible. My fluid work history and current flexible job mean I have the time and ability to accompany Pascal for his appointments and tests. One such occasion was in the spring of 2008, a little less than a year after Pascal's brain surgery. Pascal was scheduled for a checkup with his neurologists, an examination by an ophthalmologist to look for tuber growths in his eyes, and a follow-up echocardiogram to see if the tubers on his heart wall were continuing to shrink. We had a full day scheduled for us.

We got up earlier than the rest of the family and scarfed down our breakfast so that we could hit the road by 7:00am and make it safely to his 10:30am appointment. As is normal for us, we got going a bit late but not too late; we would make it just in time. It was a chilly morning on the brink of late winter and early spring. Pascal was an angel as we traversed the state routes and rural interstates that tracked us through eastern and southern Indiana on our way to the big city and the hospital. He looked at some books, took a short nap, colored a bit, and fiddled with his toy cars. We listened to the radio (when we could get a decent station in the country), and I talked about all the things we were going to do that day, including a stop for ice cream after all the appointments. We parked in the garage underneath the hospital and began our trek for the day. I took Pascal's hand and we hustled through the fume-filled parking area to one elevator, crossed the hallway to another building, and up another elevator to get to the Tuberous Sclerosis clinic. He and I were both pretty familiar with this part of the itinerary, having traveled it many times before. We knew the drill: check in, get measurements and blood pressure taken, find some toys, and wait in the examination room for a bit. We saw a few different people in the clinic that morning: neurologists and nurses, surgeons and social workers. Everyone was pleased with how well Pascal was doing after his surgery: his scar was healing well, the MRI of his brain showed good results, and we had seen a clear bump up in his development. He was a busy toddler confined to a small doctor's office and he would bop around like a super-bouncy ball, so we had a few breaks to walk around the hallway together and find some graham crackers for a snack. Pascal's doctors are skilled professionals and good people. We have come to know them well over the years, and this was a pleasant visit with lots of positive signs.

 After about an hour and a half, though, we had to scoot off to Pascal's appointment with the ophthalmologist in another section of the hospital. I took Pascal's hand and we scouted our way through the various buildings and elevators, eventually winding our way to the offices after making a few wrong turns and asking for directions a couple of times. Pascal was accustomed to holding my hand, as this was our standard operating procedure whenever we walked in public, but he did not always like it. His extraordinary impulsivity and his normal urges of toddler independence meant that sometimes I needed to grasp his hand firmly or let go and give him a small berth of freedom while we walked or waited in safer areas. After we arrived

## Holding Hands with Pascal

in the ophthalmologist's office, we had a few minutes of down time when he could play with the toys in the waiting area and I could sit and rest for a few minutes. The ophthalmologist's examination involved the rather uncomfortable process of instilling eye drops and shining a very bright light into Pascal's eye while the doctor used a special tool to look for any unusual growths. Pascal and I have been through much worse together (blood draws are a particular challenge), so this only required a moderate amount of wrestling and soothing to get Pascal still enough to finish the examination. While more uncomfortable and less familiar, this doctor had good news for us too—no eye abnormalities. We left a bit more tired than before and eager to find some lunch.

I held Pascal's hand again and we made our way down to one of the busiest areas of the hospital: the cafeteria. I thought we might have missed most of the lunch crowd (it was now just after 1pm), but we still encountered a bustling, confusing room filled with lots of choices and lines that needed to be endured with extra patience from me and extra impatience from Pascal. My dexterity and determination were put to the test while I tried to keep a firm hold on Pascal's hand in the crowd, pick out relatively healthy food for us, and then try to balance the tray on my hip without dropping anything on the floor. My senses felt like sieve spilling over because too much was being forced through too fast. As always my primary attention was on Pascal's safety, which was inextricably linked to my hold on his hand. I eventually found a sandwich and Pascal agreed to a banana and some crackers. We made it through the line and to a table. I could finally release Pascal's hand and we could simply sit next to one another while we ate, and sitting in a booth by the window was a welcome relief from the hectic cafeteria for both of us. Our conversations at this stage involved me talking simply to explain things to Pascal and sometimes in more complicated phrases out loud to myself. Pascal was in a one- to two-word phase at this point, noticing and identifying a few things in our surroundings. We felt better after having a decent meal and a little chat, and we only had one more appointment that day.

Holding Pascal's hand at this phase of his life was a very mixed experience. I had the joyful contentment of feeling his hand grip mine as I gripped his. Sometimes the joining of our hands and shared grip manifested our bond as father and son, giving us both the hopeful sense that we were in this together. Other times, Pascal acted like any other curious toddler. He would bolt off after any distraction: a fish tank here, a baby over there. What was behind that door? What is up those stairs? These would strike unexpectedly and initially generated an almost anxious sense of diligence about holding his hand. I need to be prepared for any sudden movements. Over time this has given way to a deep intuition about Pascal's notions and behaviors. I still miss things, but I have a saturating, unconscious sense of what is going on in Pascal's mind. Finally, Pascal would also actively resist me, especially when he had the sense that we were heading into another uncomfortable, or downright painful, test. He can yank so hard I think my shoulder will pop out of joint. I regularly pray that Pascal will somehow understand that my tight and unforgiving grip on his hand in these moments is still a sign of my love for him even when I am dragging him through tears (both his and mine) toward something neither of us really want to do but is ultimately for his good.

  I took Pascal's hand again and we began to walk to the cardiologist's. This was another unfamiliar location, but we found our way without problems. Pascal had a history of irregular heartbeats. He never faced severe cardiac disruption or arrest, but the irregularities needed to be tracked. These were caused by four "tubers" on his heart wall. Oddly, these tubers tend to be largest and most problematic at birth in Tuberous Sclerosis, but then they typically shrink and resolve over the years (tubers in the kidneys do the opposite). The cardiologist had more good news for us. Pascal's electrocardiogram was normal, a sign that his heart tumors were resolving and we didn't need to take any special precautions with medication or anesthesia in the future.

  We had a good day with lots of good news, but we were both exhausted. Pascal had walked on his still-stretching toddler legs for most of the day. I had walked with him holding his hand and sometimes carrying him. This was not so much a strain on my physique as it was on my psyche. My body, and particularly my hand, were tired, but my mind was completely fried from reporting details to doctors, taking in medical instructions, and always, always attending to Pascal and his safety. We were both aching to get home, so we made our way back to the car, left the hospital, and zipped over to get ice cream. I ate my peanut butter chocolate chip scoop quickly. Pascal fumbled away at his chocolate chip, and we eventually packed it up and let him finish it in the car. It was about 3 in the afternoon now, and I wanted to get home for dinnertime. We got in the car and headed out of the city. Traffic was picking up, we could get a radio station for a while, and we also had a lot to talk over from the day. The first hour or so was busy, carried along by the still-cresting tide of the energy and attention required of us all day. The car eventually settled into the hum of seventy miles per hour on the paved arrow that cut straight through the stubble strewn countryside. Our energy ebbed as the radio signals faded and we both became quiet. Pascal fell asleep for a well-deserved nap and I was left alone with my thoughts and God's presence.

My mind spun through the events of the day, a blender slowly churning pictured scenes, medical details, conversations with Pascal, hopes and fears for the future, and prayers prompted by the Spirit. In the midst of that quiet drive home, my mind caught a glimpse of a scene common in old jokes. Pascal and I were holding hands again, but we were approaching St. Peter poised at the pearly gates, welcoming people into God's kingdom. My fatigue gave the Spirit the freedom to continue to play on this image. As we came closer to the gates in my mind, I felt all of the contentment, effort, and struggle of holding Pascal's hand throughout the day compressed into the vision of that scene. As we came closer to the gates, I had no idea what to expect; I gripped Pascal's hand more tightly. We approached St. Peter who looked directly at Pascal and said, "Hi Pascal, and welcome. We've been waiting for you. Who is this with you?" Pascal answered (maybe with words, I'm not sure), "This is my dad. He's with me." Peter responded, "Oh, very good. Welcome to both of you. Please come in."

I had walked the entire day thinking that I was holding Pascal's hand, that I was the responsible one who needed to be in control, who needed to guide and protect Pascal through the destinations and complexities of the imposing hospital. This vision gave me a glimpse of how God perceives power and weakness, how God measures out value in the economy of the kingdom. Through that vision I caught a glimpse of the inversion of our values in God's perspective. The poor in spirit are blessed because God's kingdom belongs to them (Matt

# Holding Hands with Pascal

5:3). Only those who are humble like a child will enter the kingdom (Matt 18:4). The greatest among us really is the least (Luke 22:26). I was being a good father to Pascal by holding his hand through the easy and hard parts of the day, but it was not until this moment that I realized what holding hands with Pascal fully meant. God has entrusted him to my care, and I will continue to hold his hand as I follow Christ, but I also know that Pascal holds my hand and that his weakness leads me into the kingdom of God.

Maybe it's a kind of genius that makes you
seize, the tubers on your brain prodigious
visitors who ask repeatedly if we are paying

attention. Settled here among us, they pose
only the important questions. You're as much
a philosopher as the one you're named for,

little man, your tremors the minor collisions
that force us to envision and avoid a crash.
You're a prophet, slow to speak, your crooked

smile as shy as shadow, your eyes sometimes
heavy from the medicine, their faint flickers
somehow keeping every God-shaped void alit.

—"AFTER PENSEES," A POEM FOR PASCAL BRUEHLER
BY MARY M. BROWN

# 10

# The Gift of Pascal

*Now David was ruddy and had beautiful eyes and was handsome. The Lord said, "Rise and anoint him; for this is the one."*

—1 SAMUEL 16:12

PASCAL'S LIFE IS WONDERFUL. Yes, it has been marred and scarred (literally, in some cases) by his disorder and his developmental challenges, but it is no less wonderful. As the poem just before this chapter says, Pascal has a kind of genius that prompts us to ask the most important questions and keeps our hearts open to God. This is the first chapter of three that stresses the gifts given to us by God as we have held hands with Pascal—a balance to the grief present in the first half of the book. The first and foundational gift is Pascal himself, but his precarious presence "settled here among us" issues forth with many other gifts. As with the preceding chapter on my wife, Anne, I enter this chapter with an anxiety driven both by expectation and hesitation. Can I properly and responsibly enter into Pascal's life and express what it is and how he experiences it? Can I write a book about Pascal without trying to do this? I feel the warning of Stanley Hauerwas when he says, "We seek to prevent retardation not because we are inhumane but because we fear the retarded lack the means of giving and receiving empathy, and thus we cannot imagine how they

## The Gift of Pascal

feel."[1] I too lacked the Spirit-given imagination to empathize with those who have severe developmental problems until I lived so much of life holding hands with Pascal. Hauerwas is right to point out that a lack of imagination and empathy can lead us to dehumanize those with disabilities, but I have been on a journey of overcoming that for all of Pascal's life. Pascal bears a name from my grandmother and looks like my father more than anyone else in the family. He and I have been through highs and lows together, from the joys of learning to swim to the terror as he lay sick and seizing in front of me. Pascal's life and our bond has been a gift that has expanded my imagination and empathy. I do believe I can feel alongside what he feels, that he is knowable and I truly know him. He may not be able to write this chapter for himself, but I can write it for him, not out of an attempt to put him in a box but out of an attempt to pay attention, to hear his prophetic voice, and to express the inspiring wonder of his life.

I see echoes and correspondences between the life of David and Pascal, and so the story of David weaves in and out of this chapter, providing a biblical touchstone for my description of Pascal. Pascal shares some of David's good looks. You might recall how Soren put his own description of Pascal in the preface to chapter 5: "When somebody says handsome, I think of Pascal." Pascal is a good-looking kid: thick hair and a boyish face, and flecked blue eyes (like his dad). He may not be reddish-ruddy like David, but he has a pleasant skin tone that tans easily. Among these points are little signs of his disorder that appear upon closer inspection: odd rough patches on his head and face and little pockets of white skin scattered amongst his tan complexion. His face has tiny reddish bumps across his nose and cheeks. These are hard to see now, but in most folks with Tuberous Sclerosis these little tumors increase in size and color, often dramatically affecting a person's appearance, so he may come to share more of David's ruddy complexion over time. Pascal is built like a barrel with four oak-strong limbs. He is a solid, stocky guy. Pascal may not have the impressive physique of David's older brothers (see 1 Sam 16:6–7), but like David he looks handsome and healthy.

The gift of Pascal's life might be overlooked just as David was overlooked. God had to rouse Samuel and compel him to seek out a

---

1. Stanley Hauerwas, *Suffering Presence*, 174.

new king to replace Saul (1 Sam 16:1–2), and Jesse (David's father) did not even think David was old enough or important enough to invite to the sacrificial feast with Samuel (16:11). When Samuel sees David's impressive older brothers, God has to remind him: "The Lord does not see as mortals see; they look on the outward appearance, but the Lord looks on the heart" (16:7). Perhaps even more than outward appearance, today we look at a person's capacities and abilities. We judge their value by what they can do, by how they can contribute to society, much as Samuel probably thought that imposing stature meant the ability to lead and fight well. God does not look on these things that we call "productive" and "normal" but on a person's inner disposition. Hauerwas warns us that we may not think the disabled have a fully formed "heart" for God to see and judge, but I have learned that Pascal most certainly does (as do others with severe developmental problems). God doesn't look on Pascal's appearance or abilities; rather, God sees something more in Pascal's heart. As soon as David arrives, God unreservedly tells Samuel, "Rise and anoint him; for this is the one" (16:13). We trudged through many years searching for God's purpose in giving us Pascal, like Samuel reviewing all of Jesse's older sons. Only after some time did we realize what a gift Pascal is, how God had anointed him and filled him with his Spirit.

Prophets, priests, and kings—this is the classic triad of offices in the Old Testament anointed by God to lead God's people. Back in chapter 2 I compared Pascal to a priest, one who leads others in the worship of God, and seeing his life through David's life adds the dimension of king, someone who leads God's people. From our ability-biased perspective, we don't know how to fit the disabled or different into our churches, but they can and should be welcomed to take their place in the body of Christ, and even lead.[2] God has been in the habit of choosing what is weak in the eyes of the world to shame the strong for a long time (1 Cor 1:27). David was a surprise to Samuel, and that the weak and different can lead the church is a surprise to us. As David's life unfolds in the stories of Scripture, we find further comparisons that help show the character and influence of Pascal's life.

---

2. Eiesland, *Disabled God*, 82–85; and Hauerwas, *Suffering Presence*, 182–83.

## The Gift of Pascal

The classic Sunday school tale about David's life is his defeat of Goliath (1 Sam 17). David is sent by his father with some food and supplies to refresh his older brothers on the battlefield. When David arrives he hears the brazen challenge of the giant Goliath taunting the people of Israel. David asks (a couple of times) what will be done for the person who defeats Goliath, much to the consternation of his brothers (vv. 26–30). Some of the soldiers must have taken David's questioning as sign of his willingness to fight the giant, and David is taken to Saul. Pascal is a sign of weakness and difference in the midst of the church, and he poses hard questions to us—questions that make us uncomfortable. As the poem just before this chapter artfully observes, Pascal raises all the "important questions": How could God let this happen? What meaning does his life have? What should we do with the disabled? Pascal does not perceive these as insurmountable challenges. Instead, he faces them head on and lives his life with joy (and with tantrums). He fights the "giant" of his genetic disorder every day even when we are paralyzed by fear and uncertainty. Sometimes he wins and sometimes he loses, but he always poses those big questions. Pascal poses those big questions and presses on even when the answers aren't clear.

David is initially scorned by Saul: "You can't possibly fight Goliath. You're just a boy" (17:33). David goes on to list all the things he did as a shepherd, including driving off and killing lions and bears with God's protection (17:34–37). If somebody thinks Pascal can't be a functioning part of the church I can list several things God has brought him through: seizures, brain surgery, learning to use the bathroom, talking in sentences, and much more. Pascal spent two years in our church's pre-school Sunday school classroom, even though he was seven and eight during this time and was a good bit bigger than most of the other kids. The first year definitely had its bumps, and he really needed the assistance of his helper, Miss Peggy. However, during the second year we were often told Pascal had been the best-behaved child in the class that morning, that he participated enthusiastically, and he had played kindly with the other kids. Saul seems to accept David's bold claims and David tries to suit up like a real warrior with armor, helmet, and sword, but he is a dismal failure at normal warfare. He couldn't even walk let alone use the weapons properly, so he goes out against the giant with a measly sling

(17:38–40). Pascal may not operate with the words, skills, and abilities of other people, but his perseverance, his joy, and his kindness are not inferior "weapons." They are just different gifts from God. Pascal has endured intense medical interventions and therapy to improve his health and development, and we have seen his kindness for others blossom with his little sister and classmates. We might slip into thinking it was David's talents or abilities that led to his successes (see the praise of David in 16:18), and that the same is somehow true of us even if we are in Christ. Pascal's real and apparent lack of ability becomes an even clearer reminder that God has told us: "not by might, nor by power, but by my Spirit" (Zech 4:6). Pascal, in his weakness, is particularly open to God's Spirit, and what he does (and does not do) challenges us to greater openness to God and others.[3] David didn't accomplish things by his own power. Pascal doesn't accomplish things by his own power. David and Pascal remind us that we should not try to do things in our own power.

The next echo I see in Pascal's life comes from David's joyful abandon and love of music. The very first thing Scripture records after Samuel anoints David is that the young David becomes Saul's "music therapist" when Saul is troubled by a spirit sent from God (17:14–18). David is credited with setting up choirs of Levites (1 Chr 15:16), and David appears to be the singer/songwriter of many psalms (see the titles to Psalms 50–60). When David led the Ark of the Covenant into Jerusalem, he "danced before the Lord with all his might" to the sound of shouts and trumpets (2 Sam 6:14). Pascal shares David's love of music and dancing; he enjoys listening to music, and he learns the lyrics very quickly, which has definitely helped his speech development. Eleanor recently started taking Suzuki violin lessons, and Pascal is convinced he is going to start playing the drums. (Whew! That child on drums—we might need a soundproof room in the house.) Many children with special needs often struggle with over-stimulation. They can be overwhelmed by noise, movement, structure, taste, or touch, and handling with care is definitely in order. Pascal is in a minority that struggles with under-stimulation. He stomps when he walks, throws his body into couches, wants the music turned up, and dances with some pretty wild moves. And

---

3. Yong, *Theology and Down Syndrome*, 218–22.

## The Gift of Pascal

he loves, I mean absolutely loves, to swim. The pressure, feel, and motion of the water is exactly what his body craves. When he was younger Pascal and I had our daily workout, which involved putting on some loud big band jazz and going through a series of activities that an innocent observer might call professional wrestling moves: pushing heavy objects, spinning around, bear hugs, being dropped onto the couch, and so on. It was Pascal's daily "sensory diet" and it helped him be a bit more centered for the rest of the day. We often have to bring down Pascal's activity level a couple of notches to match the social situation, but he has learned to have better control over the years, and I am delighted that he can use his body to express his feelings and joy in meaningful (and safe) ways. His body, disordered as it is in its basic genetic building blocks, is still a means for him to praise his Maker. Every once in a while we turn on a favorite song and have a family dance party to celebrate or just have fun together. Music and dancing together: Pascal loves it, and I'm pretty sure God does too.

The last connection to David's life is that Pascal loves people. The early story of David's life in 1 Samuel before he becomes king repeatedly mentions his relationship with Jonathan, Saul's son. From the very moment the two men meet their souls were bound together, and they form a covenant with one another as a tangible sign of their love for one another (18:1–3). Jonathan continues to intercede for David with his father (19:1–7), and when it becomes clear Saul is intent on killing David they part, confirming their friendship with tears and commitment. Pascal is somewhere on the autism spectrum, and he does struggle with appropriate social skills. Often he doesn't look people in the eyes. Sometimes he uses his body instead of his words to get what he wants. He can be oblivious to less-than-obvious social cues. But Pascal loves people and he loves his friends. While still a bit awkward, when we have guests in our house Pascal will almost immediately take them by the hand and urge them to come join him in whatever he is currently playing. We often joke that Pascal has never met a stranger. People unfamiliar with Pascal can initially be put off by his halting speech and unclear desires, but his kindly persistence and sincerity win them over quickly. Like a fish unexpectedly jumping out of still water, he will spontaneously inquire about his friends and classmates during quiet moments: "Go see Sarah? When I see Sarah? I play tennis [with] Sarah?" Often, the first thing

Holding Hands with Pascal

out of his mouth in the morning is to ask about his beloved sibling: "Where Eleanor? Get uuuuup Eleanor!" Sleep was merely a mildly necessary interruption between playing with his friends and family. The kids who take the time to befriend Pascal benefit from his absolute love and loyalty: "Stiles's house? I want see Bradley, pleeeeease." Like David and Jonathan, leaving his friends is sad and painful, often bringing forth tears (and tantrums) that are a sign of his deep connection to these people in his life. Even with all of his developmental, speech, and socialization challenges, Pascal opens friendships with others and binds himself to other people. In his weakness and difference he reminds us how we need and long for relationships with one another, relationships that God can use to heal our souls and chase away the specter of loneliness.[4] He prophetically pokes at our shallow friendships in the body of Christ, and shows us that our weaknesses and differences should not be obstacles to loving relationships within the church and beyond its metaphorical walls.

I hope this chapter has given you a taste of the joy and wonder of Pascal's life. Pascal's life and our lives are both grief and joy. The good things do not cancel out the bad or even balance the difficulties he faces into some kind of equilibrium. Pascal's life is a mixture of good and bad all jumbled up and all redeemed by God. With David, Pascal can grieve in his soul and feel sorrow all day long (Ps 13:2 and 32:3), but as with so many of the psalms the story does not end with grief and pain but with rejoicing, and with David, Pascal rejoices and sings over God's abundant goodness (Ps 13:5–6 and 32:11).

## Discussion Questions:

1. Samuel says Saul's successor will be "a man after God's own heart" (1 Sam 13:14). Drawing from this chapter and other parts of the book, how would you say Pascal is a person "after God's own heart"?
2. What "important questions" does Pascal's life pose? How has this book led you to rethink disability and weakness?

4. Jean Vanier explains how both the residents and assistants in L'Arche communities are transformed through loving relationships (Hauerwas and Vanier, *Living Gently*, 25–28).

3. Most of us experience weakness and difference as causes of sadness and separation. How can they become opportunities for joy and a new openness to God's Spirit?

4. Pascal expresses his joy in his weakness, with his body, and with his friends. What are the sources of joy in your life and how do you express them?

# 11

## The Gift of a Sister

*Be merciful, just as your Father is merciful.*
—LUKE 6:36

IF OUR FAMILY LIFE is like a banana split with different flavors of ice cream (that not everybody likes), a few kinds of toppings (some would prefer less), with whipped cream and nuts (that some want and others don't) all jumbled together in a sprawling bowl that everyone has to share, then Eleanor is the cherry on top. She is the cute, sweet note placed on top right at the end, and everybody agrees she makes the whole sundae just look and feel right. Her cheerful and merciful spirit is exactly what our family needed.

After Pascal was a few years old, Anne and I began to talk and pray about having another child. We had always mused about having three kids, but we asked ourselves whether that was another dream that had to be shelved in light of Pascal's struggles. We thought of adopting, but we know adopted children can bring a host of special issues. Could we handle that alongside the demands of Pascal's needs? Pascal's disorder was genetic. Anne and I were both tested for the disorder, and the tests came back negative, but there was always a risk of the test being wrong or not testing the proper cells in our bodies. Aside from Tuberous Sclerosis, we faced the whole host of other possibilities that now seemed more real and threatening than before: birth defects, other disorders, health problems, etc. Was it foolish to try to have another child? Shouldn't we focus our love and energy on Soren and Pascal?

In the end, two factors swayed us to try to have another child together. The first was a conviction that more kids didn't mean less love to go around but more love to go around. God's love does not diminish in quantity or character because it is shared amongst the members of the Trinity. On the contrary, we believe that the reciprocal love of the Father, Son, and Spirit flows over into all creation. Jesus invites us to come and share with him in the love of God, and so he prayed to God, "That the love with which you loved me may be in them, and I in them" (John 17:26). We don't dispense love out of some limited pool; together we share in God's overflowing love. The more people who share it the more God's love redounds, so having another child would bring more love and life to our family. We also began to think of the long term, to a time when we would be older and then gone. Pascal has continued to progress well, but his health or development could stall or take a turn for the worse unexpectedly. We looked ahead to a time when the responsibility to care for Pascal might fall to Soren, and we did not want to leave him to bear that burden alone. So, we thought another sibling would be a gift to Soren, a friend and support for him and Pascal as our children moved into life and maturity without us.

These were good reasons, and God used them to prompt us to have another child together, but as is God's way, so many unexpected blessings were in store for us all. Our little Eleanor was born small but healthy, and much to our relief there were no signs of Tuberous Sclerosis (or any other problems). The first few months were trying. Combine all the needs of a newborn, a very tired mommy and daddy, Pascal's continued needs, along with Soren's ever-sensitive psyche and you've got quite a stressful household. In time we settled into new habits as a family of five, and we began to see some of the gifts God has sent us with Eleanor. I wrote earlier about the extremes our two boys represent: Pascal is delayed and rough while Soren is bright and sensitive. Eleanor turned out to be quite the happy medium. Soren hit all of his developmental milestones early (walking at eleven months), Pascal hit all of his late (didn't walk until about twenty months), but Eleanor was right in the normal range. She "walked" scuffing around on her knees for a while, but then started toddling around on a fairly predictable schedule. Soren and Pascal both seem prone to emotional outbursts (Pascal to tantrums and Soren to tears), but Eleanor was a delightfully happy baby and toddler. We joked that we might think about having another child if we could guarantee that our next baby would have the same demeanor as Eleanor. Eleanor is now four and she has her moments too—very temperamental when she wakes up from a nap—but she continues to be the happy medium of our family. No matter who is upset with whom at any given time, everybody wants to be around Eleanor. She gets along with everybody, plays with everybody, and listens to everybody. Her cheerful and kind playfulness is like a release from the gravity that sometimes seems to cause us all to crash into one another.

While Soren was in the forefront of our minds when we decided to have Eleanor, she has been a blessing to Pascal in ways we never imagined, and here we come to the verse cited at the beginning of the chapter. Once we were pretty sure we were having a girl (Anne's pregnancy side effects were totally different this time around), we started to search for a name that would bear up alongside Soren and Pascal. Let me tell you that knowing a few ancient languages (as I do) really throws a wrench into reading baby name books. Most sources say Eleanor comes from a Greek word for "light." Well, I know Greek (ancient Greek anyway), and no Greek word for light looks anything like "Eleanor." What "Eleanor" most resembles is the verb *eleaō*, which means "to have mercy." This (and a bit of inspiration from Eleanor Roosevelt) convinced us this would be a great name for our child, and it turned out to be quite fitting because of all the ways Eleanor has brought the gift of mercy to our home. In Scripture, mercy carries two connotations. First, mercy bears a strong emotional dimension. To have mercy is to feel compassion or to be moved by concern for another person. Paul says God "had mercy" on him by preserving the life of Epaphroditus and sparing Paul another sorrow. We hear in Luke 1:78 of God's "tender mercies," a common phrase sometimes translated as the "bowels of mercy" in the King James Version (see Phil 2:1 and Col 3:12). This phrase captures the ancient (and sometimes contemporary) notion that compassion and pity is felt in our "guts," that this deep emotional reaction yanks at the

*The Gift of a Sister*

pit of our stomachs. Second, mercy is also tied to concrete actions of helping others generated by this heartfelt concern. God has mercy on Elizabeth and enables her to conceive a child (Luke 1:58). By his mercy, God gives us a new hope through Christ (1 Pet 1:3). The Good Samaritan "showed mercy" by helping the beaten and robbed traveler (Luke 10:37). In the words of Luke 6:36, Eleanor is merciful just as God is merciful. You can tell she loves and cares for her brothers. She wants to be around them and gets emotionally involved when they are upset or hurt. She will often ask us, "Why [is] Pascal crying?" because she wants to know what is wrong with her dear brother. She also shows this in little acts of mercy. She runs to greet Pascal when he gets out of school, she brings pens or toys to Soren, and she cries and laughs with them when they need it most. God has granted Eleanor the gift of mercy, and that gift spills over to us all every day through her sweet spirit and kind deeds.

Right after the command to be merciful in Luke 6:36, Jesus follows up with another directive: "Do not judge" (6:37). Sometimes in our modern world filled with experiences and media images of evil and moral decay we wonder how it is that we should not judge. Eleanor models this perfectly in our family, because even at four years of age I don't think she has any conception that something could be wrong with Pascal. Soren is acutely aware of Pascal's challenges and problems, but Eleanor has not recognized or "judged" Pascal's condition. One of the repercussions of projects aimed at the disabled as well as the language used to discuss disability is that they come laden with assumptions made by "healthy" and "abled" people. To be "dis-abled" is to not be able, to not be like the rest of us, and while medical and therapeutic advances have done wonders for Pascal and many others, we are still aiming to make these very different people into some idealized "able" persons. We have judged the disabled to be unlike us, and we have set out on a (very compassionate) program to make them more like us. This has been called the cult of normalcy or the bias of "ableism."[1] Eleanor has no such prejudice at all, for she has not judged Pascal to be unlike her, unlike any of us. He is just who he is with his problems, challenges, quirks, and gifts. Thus, Eleanor extends mercy to Pascal and is a gift to him because she sees him as

---

1. Reynolds, *Vulnerable Communion*, 52–53.

her beloved brother, not as a boy with developmental delays and a genetic disorder. He is free to flourish with her in a way he can't with most everyone else.

On the flip side of this and on the flip side of Luke 6:36, we find another way in which Eleanor has shown mercy to Pascal. In the lead up to the command to be merciful as our Father is merciful, Jesus gives us some examples of what that looks like. We are to love our enemies and lend to people without expecting anything in return (6:35). Jesus urges us away from a contractual valuation of our relationships (even our business relationships it seems!). One of our primary judgments against the "disabled" is that they do not have the capacity to respond to us or do not have the capacity to contribute to society or to the church. They are disabled precisely because they do not have the ability to give in return. Two things have gone sour here. First, we have misjudged or underestimated the gifts of those who are weak and different among us. We expect to get repaid "in kind," and so we miss the gifts of love and kindness the weakest among us give in return. Second, we fail to see that all giving and receiving happens within God's economy, for the end of Luke 6:35 tells us if we give to those who are unable to repay us we do still have a reward: we "will be children of the Most High." In an even better image, Jesus instructs us to invite the "poor, crippled, lame, and blind" to banquets in our homes, and since they cannot repay us, we will be "repaid at the resurrection of the righteous" (Luke 14:13-14). Jesus instructs us to make the weak and different a part of the inner circle of our friends, guests in our homes. Eleanor welcomes Pascal in this way every day, for she loves him without condition and with no expectation for compensation. Eleanor and Pascal do have their tiffs, but this is only part of the process of two human beings learning to love one another. One of her most merciful habits is how she weaves Pascal into her life in a hundred little ways: "Hi Pascal! Come play [with] me, Pascal! Chase me, Pascal!" More than anyone else (even me, I think), he is bound to her, feels welcomed by her, knows he is home with her. This is what it means to not judge and to show mercy.

Pascal was going through a rather rough patch when he was between four and five. While his brain surgery had completely eliminated the clusters of partial seizures he had as a toddler, he became vulnerable to dramatic seizures that would strike infrequently and

*The Gift of a Sister*

were very difficult to treat. At the same time, his sleeping patterns were out of whack and his behavior had gotten more impulsive and overactive. Some of this may have been due to what doctors call "forced normalization." This occurs when seizures are controlled through some means (surgery, medicine, diet) so that the brain now has no outlet for the negative or disruptive forces that used to come out in seizures; some people experience depression or hyperactivity as a side effect of controlled seizures. This was another rocky time for us as a family. Eleanor was still a baby, Pascal's behavior was very difficult to handle, and Soren's emotions were raw and exposed. Thankfully, a few things came together in the next year. We found an appropriate mix of medication that helped Pascal settle into regular sleep habits. Through some conversations and exploration, Pascal became eligible for Applied Behavior Analysis therapy (often used with children on the autism spectrum) that has been very helpful for his development and behavior. He also started on his high-fat, low-carb diet that successfully controlled his seizures.

But the cherry on top was Eleanor. As she blossomed into a toddler, she came right alongside Pascal as they both hit some developmental stages. She was two, going on three, and Pascal was developmentally about three when his health and behavior ceased to be insurmountable obstacles for him. It was perfect timing and perhaps the best gift Pascal has ever been given. They were learning the same things at the same time and learning them all the better *together*. Eleanor was passing through that amazing phase when babbling and first words start to turn into the precious communication of a toddler. Sounds, words, and sentences started to come together like a picture you didn't know you were doodling but suddenly appears to you. Pascal's speech development had been at a plateau of two words for over a year: "ball, please" or "more cheese." But as Eleanor's language sparked, so did his because they babbled, talked, and imitated each other all the time. They were both talking in sentences with each other. Eleanor has always been quieter and shyer than our boys, but it was her friendship with Pascal that helped them both learn how to be with others. Pascal often had trouble playing and sharing with other kids due to his limited communication and impulsive reactions. They began a little game of coloring the same picture together (flowers, animals, etc.), and Eleanor was simply delighted to give crayons to

99

her brother or to swap coloring books: "Pascal, you want red," and "Pascal, I trade [with] you?" Trading, sharing, and working together became their norm. Now, they do argue quite often, and I say they argue like two old men, quibbling endlessly over some irrelevant point: "Sky is cloudy." Then, "No, no clouds, sunny." Back and forth, back and forth they go. They often return to laughing together (sometimes parental mediation is required), but again Eleanor has taught Pascal to argue and make up, something we could all use some lessons on. These daily habits and interactions have helped Pascal learn to be with others in ways that are both honest and generous. Eleanor has helped Pascal come out to other people with the kindness and friendship he had learned from his sister.

Eleanor was exactly what Pascal needed at just the right time in his life, and she will be a friend to him for years to come. She has shown and taught our entire family a bit of what it means to be merciful as God is merciful.

## Discussion Questions:

1. What is your understanding of the word "mercy"? How can we be merciful as God is merciful? Describe a time when you truly saw someone both feel and show mercy.

2. How can we wisely and practically refrain from judging others? How do our assumptions of what is "normal" get in the way of this?

3. Have you ever served or given to someone whom you thought could not repay you? Why did you do it, and did you find that you received something unexpected from God in return?

4. Has the Spirit ever sent an "Eleanor" into your life—a person who befriended and had mercy on you when you needed it most? Share that story.

5. How can you show mercy to those who are weak and different in your church and community?

# 12

## The Gift of Weakness

*My grace is sufficient for you, for my power is made perfect in weakness.*

—2 CORINTHIANS 12:9

WEAKNESS IS A GIFT? Isn't weakness a problem? Doesn't Jesus scold his disciples by telling them that the weakness of their flesh ruins the willingness of the spirit (Matt 26:41)? Doesn't Samson lose God's anointing by allowing Delilah to make him weak like all other men (Judg 16)? Aren't we commanded to "lift your drooping hands and strengthen your weak knees" (Heb 12:12)? And that is merely a sample of what we find in Scripture. Our contemporary American culture sees weakness as a threat to human flourishing, both corporately and individually. We aggressively treat mental and physical illnesses to diminish or reverse their weakening effects. We do SWOT analyses (strengths, weaknesses, opportunities, threats) to further develop the strengths of institutions and ameliorate the weaknesses that we identify. We fear weaknesses and resist them. Weakness is something to eliminate, an attack on regular God-given health and function. Weakness is frustrations, flaws, and failures. How can weakness be a gift?

## Holding Hands with Pascal

We might be tempted to continue to think in this way if it were not for the countercultural teaching of Paul and Jesus about weakness. Very simply, weakness creates space for the grace and power of God to flow into and through our lives. God's power is made perfect in weakness because human weakness creates the opportunity for faith to open up lives to God, allowing the grace of God to enter into persons and situations in ways that are more thorough and profound than any other means available. Weakness is the ultimate means of grace. Pascal's life provides ample examples of this, for the weaknesses of his body, his spirit, and his relationships all have created opportunities for God's grace to fill our lives.

Physical weakness dominated Pascal's infancy and early childhood, primarily through the seizures that plagued him. Parents in the epilepsy community often speak of the scary "seizure monster" that stalks their child. Pascal's first seizure monster was more like a doppelganger that we couldn't identify. It was sneaky and would strike unexpectedly with mysterious and troubling results. We fought off this one with medication. The next seizure monster was more like a swarm of insects, a series of little quivers that individually were not terrible, but they came on Pascal in debilitating clusters that put him in a haze. We were able to repel this monster with surgery. The most recent seizure monster was more like an ogre. Huge, crushing convulsions would overtake Pascal in one blow with life-threatening results. A special diet beat this last one back. Throughout this time our eyes and energies were focused on finding medical parries to ward off the physical effects of Pascal's seizures. Our responses were fixated on his body—the immediate point of need.

It is only now in hindsight that I can look back and see all the ways God's grace poured into our lives through those physical weaknesses. Paul looked back on his life and saw this as well. Paul tells the Galatians, "You know that it was because of a physical infirmity that I first announced the gospel to you; though my condition put you to the test, you did not scorn or despise me, but welcomed me as an angel of God, as Christ Jesus" (Gal 4:13–14). Paul speaks of a "physical infirmity"—literally a "weakness of the flesh"—as the *cause* of his preaching to the Galatians.[1] It was only because of Paul's weak-

---

1. The exact nature of Paul's "weakness" is unknown. Paul's comments in v. 15 ("you would have torn out your eyes and given them to me") have led some

*The Gift of Weakness*

ness that the gospel came to the Galatians. Paul acknowledges our deep human revulsion to weakness, for Paul's weakness "tested" the Galatians. They were tempted to reject Paul and the gospel because of this very weakness, and yet it became the occasion for them to graciously welcome Paul with a degree of honor and kindness that elevated him far above his weak status. Pascal's physical problems have allowed us to be kindly welcomed across the years by family and friends, doctors and therapists, and sometimes by brothers and sisters in Christ. As we have experienced welcome by so many people we have had a taste of God's gracious welcome that is extended to everyone through Jesus. Paul also explains to the Corinthians that he came to them "in weakness and in fear and in much trembling" (1 Cor 2:3). This seems to have enabled a proclamation of the gospel that was a "demonstration of the Spirit and of power" so that their faith might rest "on the power of God" (1 Cor 2:4-5). Again, weakness makes room for the activity of God's Spirit and allows faith to have its proper object, the gracious power of God. I pray we have shared some morsel of God's grace with those who have welcomed us in the midst of trying circumstances and that our weakness has drawn attention to God's powerful presence with us.

Many of Pascal's weaknesses are rooted in his physical condition, the genetic disorder that impacts every cell of his body, but they go on to encompass much of his growth and life. Doctors identify this as "pervasive developmental delay," a catch-all diagnosis that indicates how Pascal's development is slower across the board in several domains than other children his age (without assigning any cause to it). Pascal shows marked delays in his speaking, social skills, mental acuity, large and fine motor development, executive functioning, and other areas. The medical profession gauges this diagnosis on scales of development, which can be both good and harmful. It can be harmful to put Pascal in a disabled box based on what is "typical" or "normal," when those standards vary and when that label can be used to demean or discriminate. It can be good to identify that Pascal does have special needs we as parents and friends should attend to

---

to suggest that this was a chronic eye or vision problem. This may or may not be the same weakness or "thorn" that Paul refers to in 2 Corinthians. Paul's experience of disability may have shaped his theological perspective on weakness (Yong, *The Bible*, 83–87).

and care for. Pascal is lacking abilities and capacities that most people have, and he will face unusual challenges because of that. We see this overall, life-encompassing weakness mentioned in Scripture as well. I believe this is what Jesus is speaking of when he calls the "poor in spirit" blessed at the beginning of the Beatitudes (Matt 5:3). Most of the Beatitudes work with a very countercultural kind of logic. We do not seek out occasions to mourn as a means to blessing. The meek are the last people we expect to rule over the earth. How can the persecuted rejoice and be glad? Jesus puts the "poor in spirit" first in this list of blessings because they are the last people we think of—the people who are insignificant, ignorable, who play no meaningful role in the world because of their weakness and their poverty. Jesus addresses them *first* and calls them blessed because the kingdom of heaven itself belongs to them. Pascal is behind other kids his age; he is lacking many abilities others have. He can easily be overlooked (when he isn't having a tantrum!) and left out, but Jesus declares him to be blessed because the kingdom is his.

Similarly in Mark 10:14, Jesus says, "Let the little children come to me; do not stop them; for it is to such as these that the kingdom of God belongs." We often read this as an exhortation from Jesus for us to have "childlike faith," since children are trusting and innocent, but this does not fit with the view of children in the ancient world or with the surrounding context in Mark. Children in much of the ancient world of Jesus and Paul were viewed as somewhat less than fully human. With male adults as the norm, children were "delayed" and "disabled," for they were both in need of special care and were not yet able to participate productively in society.[2] The surrounding context of Mark 10:14 supports this. Several stories sandwiched between two predictions of Jesus' death (9:30–32 and 10:32–34) imply that Jesus identified children as vulnerable, weak, and in need. The example of a child pushes back the disciples' desire to be great and powerful, for only those who welcome the weak and least are welcoming Jesus (9:33–37). Children appear to be particularly prone to being led astray, so if you put a stumbling block before "one of these little ones," you are culpable of a very grave crime (9:42). Divorce is one of the greatest threats to children for they are dependent on their

---

2. See the discussion of the low view of children in chapter 2 of *When Children Became People* by O. M. Bakke.

## The Gift of Weakness

parents and family to protect and raise them (10:1-12). Finally, even though the rich man had kept all of the commandments "since his childhood" (10:20), he had come to rely on his wealth rather than on God and could not give up what he had and follow Jesus (10:22). Jesus has to remind his "children" how hard it is to enter the kingdom (10:24) apart from the infinite possibilities of God (10:27). Jesus presents children as needy and vulnerable, and it is precisely people like this who will enter the kingdom of God (10:15).

Pascal is a child plus he has special needs, needs that will most likely follow him into adulthood. Jesus saw in children the vulnerability and neediness that make people open to the coming kingdom of God, and I believe he sees a double dose of those qualities in Pascal. I hope this is not labeling Pascal in a way that makes him "needy" only insofar as we think he is less than others. I am trying to follow Jesus' startling inversion of values and power to say Pascal actually has qualities we should seek to emulate. His weakness is a gift to him and to all of us. Pascal's difficulties are often a distressing disguise for the gifts of his weakness. He has had a lot of painful medical procedures and he experiences an unusual degree of frustration because of his limitations, but he has a sense of his own need and God's provision. The story of Jesus calming the storm has stuck with him more than any other episode in the gospels. He sometimes utters pieces of the story or repeats sing-song bits of the scene always with the punch line "Jesus save me in the boat." He knows Jesus is present in the storm to save those people in the boat; he is in that boat, and Jesus saves him. Because of his weaknesses Pascal has learned how to trust others who care for him, to be patient when times are hard, to be gentle with others who are weak. The challenge for us is to see through his distressing disguise to the weakness Jesus holds up as a model for all of us so we may see ourselves as weak before God and thus become the kind of people who enter the kingdom through God's ever-possible help.

Pascal's weakness has a social dimension as well because he is part of our family, part of our community, and part of our church. Pascal's weaknesses can put him at a disadvantage when it comes to meeting new people and making friends. He is sometimes overwhelmed by a social situation, and he doesn't have the typical body language and speech we use to form new relationships. His lack of inhibitions may at times be a vulnerability we have to guard, but he seeks out people to play with and befriend without the social mores that sometimes stand in our way. People are often taken aback by Pascal's friendliness. Some are troubled by this forward little boy, but many receive his hand and requests to join in games and fun. Pascal's difficulties have made it harder at times for him and for us as a family to build new relationships, but in this case both Jesus and Paul agree that weakness is a necessary component to a healthy church.

Matthew takes Jesus' comments on "becoming like little children" and places them in the midst of one of his five great collections of Jesus' teaching—the one on the church in Matthew 18. In fact, the story of Jesus taking a child and placing her in the midst of the disciples as an example of humility leads off Jesus' discussion of the nature of Christian community (vv. 1–5). Humility seems to be the foundational component of the community of disciples. Jesus then pronounces woes on those who cause these little ones to stumble (vv. 6–7). He moves on to warn the disciples: "Take care that you do not despise one of these little ones" (v. 10). Then he tells the parable of the lost sheep, reminding the church it is God's will that "not one of these little ones should be lost" (v. 14). Thus, God calls the Christian community to special care for those with special needs. Paul tells the church at Corinth, "The eye cannot say to the hand, 'I have no need of you . . .' On the contrary, the members of the body that seem to be weaker are indispensable, and those members of the body that we think less honorable, we clothe with greater honor" (1 Cor 12:21–23). Note that Paul says some people/parts "seem" to be weaker. Our human evaluation of people with disabilities marks them as weaker, less able, less honorable, but these "weaker" members of the body of Christ are actually the indispensable, the absolutely necessary parts of the church.[3] Just as Jesus' physical body has been eternally marked by glorious weakness, so that weakness must be borne by someone, must be someone's cross in our shared path of following Christ. Jesus and Paul use different metaphors, but their point seems to be the same: the church cannot exist as God wants it to without weakness. It is no accident that Paul inserts his discussion of love in 1 Corinthians 13 right in the middle of his discussion of the body of Christ and spiritual gifts. The weak and vulnerable are especially open to

---

3. Yong, *The Bible*, 91–93; and Hauerwas and Vanier, *Living Gently*, 74.

*The Gift of Weakness*

the love of God and so become conduits and models of that love for others. They have the gift that stands above, beneath, and beyond all other gifts. They live out the more excellent way of love as a model for and testimony against those who would prioritize performance and power. Likewise, welcome and forgiveness, the constituent activities of the church in Matthew 18, are not possible apart from weakness. Weakness is a gift from God that, though shared by all, stands out in a few, and that gift makes it possible for us to become the church, the living body of Christ in this world.

Jesus showed us that the weakness of a child is the pattern for those who would receive the kingdom. Paul eventually realized that God's power was more real, more perfect in his weakness and suffering than at any other moment. Pascal has embodied that weakness in our midst and given us the opportunity to learn the lessons weakness has to offer. Weakness of body, of spirit, and of society is a gift, for through it we find that God's grace and love are with us in ways that we never imagined.

## Discussion Questions:

1. What was your initial response to this chapter? Did you find weakness as a gift hard to swallow? What are your beliefs and assumptions about the nature of weakness?

2. Read Mark 10:13-16 and Matthew 18:1-5. Put in your own words what Jesus was trying to communicate by using children as the example of those who will enter the kingdom. How does your own life match up with this example?

3. Paul's experience of weakness probably shaped his perspective on God's presence in weakness. What are your experiences of weakness and how have they shaped your view of God?

4. Read 1 Corinthians 1:18-2:5. Make a list of all the ways God upends human values and expectations. What are the cultural values of our day that need to be challenged by this "gospel of weakness" found in Jesus Christ?

Grant, O Lord, that I may conform myself to your will just as I am, and that since I am ill, I may glorify you in my sufferings. I am not able to come to glory without them, and even you, my Savior, desired to reach glory only through your sufferings. You were recognized by your disciples because of the signs of your sufferings, and by sufferings you will also recognize your disciples.

Unite me to yourself; fill me with yourself and with your Holy Spirit. Enter into my heart and soul to bear my sufferings with me and to continue to live out in me the sufferings that must fill up your own passion. May you complete in your people the perfect realization of your own body, so that, filled with you, it is no longer I who live and suffer, but you who live and suffer in me, my Savior. And so sharing in some small part of your sufferings, you will fill me entirely with the glory that suffering brought to you, the glory that you share with the Father and the Holy Spirit forever and ever. Amen.

—"A Prayer to Ask God for the Proper Use of Sickness," section XV by Blaise Pascal

# 13

# Where Everything Is Going

*And the leaves of the tree are for the healing of the nations.*
—REVELATION 22:2

THE RETURN OF JESUS and God's grand renewal of creation through the Spirit is real to me, but for a long time it wasn't realistic. I knew and believed Jesus would return at God's command to defeat evil, usher in the final judgment, and pave the way for God's joyful reunion with humanity, but the thought of Jesus' return was like a loud train hurtling down its tracks right behind your house, blaring its horn. At first you can hear nothing else, but after hundreds of episodes even this engulfing sensory event settles into the din of the background noise; you hardly even know that it is there. The second coming of Jesus may be the most important event in the history of creation, but it felt remote—the bellowing trumpet is hard to hear, the cadres of angels have long been waiting, and life here goes on in numbing normalcy. I knew it was real, but I couldn't fit it into the reality I experienced on a daily basis. That changed for me with the initial crisis and chronic manifestations of Pascal's disorder, because my own son expresses the very groaning of creation for the glory that will be realized when God sets the world free from its bondage to decay (Rom 8:20–22). I now have a constantly changing, very personal, and profoundly complex reason to anticipate the return of Christ. This chapter will explore how holding hands with Pascal has illuminated what that new beginning will be like.

Much of the New Testament stretches us between productive work for the kingdom of God in the present and consuming anticipation for the realization of the kingdom of God in the future. The apostles are reprimanded for staring up into the sky after the ascended Jesus, taking their eyes off the pressing task of bearing witness (Acts 1:11), but Paul urges the Corinthians to avoid major changes in their marital status, for "the appointed time has grown short" (1 Cor 7:27–29). This tension is captured well in the parable of the talents (Matt 25:14–30). The parable opens with a wealthy householder divvying out portions of his capital to three different slaves. Then he goes away. Two of the slaves do well and double their holdings, but one hides the money in the ground out of fear. The master returns *"after a long time"* (v. 19) and settles accounts with the slaves. Their performance with their "talents" determines their destiny: the first two are given greater authority but the last is consigned to the outer darkness. We currently live in the midst of that "long time." We must keep that future reckoning in mind, but we also must be mindful to be active with what we have in the present. This is a hard balance to maintain, but holding hands with Pascal has helped me do it.

Pascal bears in his body and behavior a sliver of evidence that something has gone wrong with this world God has made. One strand of his genes is mismatched, and the effects ripple through his body and life. His behavior and growth falter and fall in ever-changing ways, so I am regularly reminded that something is amiss in this world, that something is awry and needs to be set right by God. This is where my perspective on the end and my perspective on Pascal coalesce in a way that makes both healthier. I am extremely grateful for the medical advances and therapy services that have made life better for Pascal. We will continue to pursue these with initiative and perseverance, for we believe we must help him to do all in life he can just as the slaves must develop the talents bestowed upon them. And yet, I do not want to slowly adopt the disparaging attitude of that last slave who knew his master was harsh and feared what might happen (vv. 24–25). While treatments and therapy provide traction for Pascal to thrive, I do not want to come to see Pascal merely as

## Where Everything Is Going

something broken that needs to be fixed or even cured, constantly fixating on the *dis*abilities that must be addressed. I aim instead "to enter into the joy" of our master (vv. 21, 23) with Pascal when this long time is over and the last great day has come. The master rewards his servants in kind: they were faithful with a "few things" here and share authority over "many things" in the future (v. 21). I have some degree of responsibility to steward Pascal's differences, weaknesses, and vulnerabilities, but I have a glimpse that these will somehow overflow into that future day as well. I hope to do everything I can for Pascal in this world, while always remembering this world is not everything, but everything is headed toward God's goal of renewal and recreation. I will do everything I can for Pascal, knowing God will make things right in ways I cannot imagine. I will participate in fruitful work in this world, knowing Jesus is returning to bring both renewal and reward.

How do we get from here to there, from this present persistence to that future reality? We walk the path of weakness and suffering. Scripture is shot through with this principle: the Israelites face many years of wandering in the desert before they reach the promised land; God's people have to face the exile prophesied in chapters 1–39 of Isaiah before they can receive the comfort promised in chapters 40–66 of Isaiah; Jesus must endure death on the cross before he is exalted by God (Phil 2:6–11). And "it is through many troubles that we must enter the kingdom of God" (Acts 14:22). Blaise Pascal (our Pascal's namesake) recognized this in the midst of his own illness, and crafted a long prayer asking God that he might use the occasion of his weakness rightly. The end of that prayer is cited just before this chapter, and in it Pascal prays that he might travel the same path Jesus did from suffering to ultimate glory. As it draws to a close, his prayer is even more audacious, for he asks that he might suffer with Jesus and that Jesus would suffer in him so he may also share the very glory Jesus shares with the Father and the Holy Spirit. Suffering and weakness are opportunities to be united with Jesus, and the Jesus who suffered is the same Jesus who is glorified. As we hold hands with Pascal in his suffering, we are simultaneously holding hands with Jesus who suffered. Jesus' suffering led him to glory in God's plan. We can walk that path with Pascal as well.

## Holding Hands with Pascal

As we contemplate that ultimate glory, we return to a topic raised at the beginning of the book in chapter 2 on "How Everything Really Started." The way we think about the future glory and recreation of the world impacts how we act in the present. If disabling conditions like genetic disorders and autism as well as acquired disabilities such as blindness and paralysis have no place in the new heaven and new earth, then it would be natural to seek to eliminate them here in this world as well. The problem is that if heaven has no disabled people, then perhaps our churches will quietly exclude or marginalize disabled people since they do not fit into our vision of God's ultimate reality.[1] To put that conclusion this baldly makes it sound patently false, and yet we maintain the pervasive belief that the new creation will be devoid of the weaknesses that characterize this life. Several passages of Scripture push back and make it difficult to continue to hold onto this perspective.

First, we have the example of the body of Jesus discussed back in chapter 2. Jesus' body clearly and obviously retains the physical wounds of the resurrection; they are available and open for Thomas to insert his fingers and hand into (John 20:26–29). Only by showing his hands and feet (with their wounds) is Jesus able to convince the disciples he is not some kind of apparition (Luke 24:39). Revelation, in its opening throne room vision, presents Jesus as the lamb that was slaughtered standing in the midst of the worship of heaven. If Jesus himself bears the marks of his suffering into eternity as signs of his identity and of the power of God at work with him, then will we not do the same? Jesus is our model and pattern; what happens to Jesus happens to us. Jesus suffers and we suffer with him (1 Pet 2:21). Jesus dies and we die with him (Rom 6:4–5). Jesus is raised and we are raised with him (Col 3:1). Jesus reigns and we reign with him (Rev 22:5). If Jesus bears some of the marks of his suffering and weakness on this earth, then we can expect to do the same. Those wounds and marks of weakness are at the core of our God-given identity and have been the occasion for the demonstration of God's power and grace in this world that will carry over into heaven. If people of all kinds of nations, tribes, peoples, and languages stand before God and the Lamb declaring God's glory (Rev 7:9–10), then surely people of all

---

1. Yong, *The Bible*, 120–22.

## Where Everything Is Going

kinds of bodies will be there as well, testifying by their voices and their beings to the amazing nature of God's salvation.

Paul presents us with several images to explain that these new bodies will both somehow be like our current bodies and somehow unlike our current bodies. He speaks of physical bodies and spiritual bodies, but they are both bodies (1 Cor 15:44). We will be changed: the perishable will put on imperishability, and the mortal will put on immortality (15:53–54). Yet doesn't Paul say this is "sown in weakness, but raised in power" (15:43)? Does that not presume that all these things we call "weaknesses" will be overcome and sloughed off in that new life? Yes, in some respect this is true, but not in ways we might think. When Paul speaks of perishability, dishonor, and weakness in 1 Corinthians 15 he is primarily speaking of the way in which our current bodies are subject to death. The return of the resurrected Jesus is the final defeat of death: "Death has been swallowed up in victory" (15:54). Pascal faces weaknesses bent toward death such as dangerous impulsivity and the drastic seizures that wrack his brain. I believe God will remove these things (and other, similar deadly symptoms) that cause us tears and mourning, for there will be no more death when the first things pass away (Rev 21:4). Other weaknesses will be maintained in the continuity of our bodies, for "we have this treasure in clay jars, so that it may be clear that this extraordinary power belongs to God" (2 Cor 4:7). Our weaknesses in this world are like transparent and transient containers that help reveal the presence of God's grace and goodness. The transient nature of our current "tent" will be replaced by another, more enduring building provided by God in the new age (2 Cor 5:1); we should not yearn to be "unclothed"—that is, devoid of all weakness—but even further clothed so that those weaknesses may more permanently and more perfectly reveal the life of God in us (2 Cor 5:4). That new building from God will enshrine those weaknesses that reveal God's grace while undoing the ones that cause death. The Spirit who helps us in our current weakness (Rom 8:26) is the guarantee of this future existence, an existence in which the distressing disguise of Pascal's disorder will no longer be distressing or a disguise but a consummate reflection of the life, love, and power of God.

On a broader scale, I believe this same reality persists in the new heaven and earth on the basis of a line in Revelation 22. We often think of the recreated universe as a place of stasis where perfection is enacted and maintained for all eternity, but Revelation 22:1-2 speaks to a different kind of existence:

> Then the angel showed me the river of the water of life, bright as crystal, flowing from the throne of God and of the Lamb through the middle of the street of the city. On either side of the river is the tree of life with its twelve kinds of fruit, producing its fruit each month; and the leaves of the tree are for the healing of the nations.

The water of the river of life is constantly flowing, emerging from God the author of life, and gushing out into the midst of the city. The tree of life is there as well, but not in suspended animation. The tree of life is fruitful, producing fruit on some kind of regular monthly timetable. The leaves grow as well, for the healing of the nations. Healing of the nations? What remains to be healed? Wasn't everything healed, completely restored at the arrival of the new heaven and earth? While John does not expand on the details or reasons here, we see that God continues healing for all eternity. This final scene of Revelation portrays God's life-giving, productive, restoring, and healing activity going on for all eternity for all people. We are still the objects of God's grace and still continue to generate praise as God's infinite life is manifested through our existence, which stands in eternal need of God's healing power.

Pascal's weaknesses are not all anomalies to be fought against, flaws that will be undone and eradicated when Jesus comes to set up God's kingdom on earth. Much to the contrary, his weaknesses teach us to value our own weaknesses as those points of our existence where we walk with Christ most closely as we begin the process of being conformed to his image (Rom 8:29). In our weakness, we suffer with him, and in the end we will be glorified with him (8:30). Many of our weaknesses are not the most transient parts of this "earthly tent" that are passing away. No, they are the most permanent parts of our being granted to us as gifts that enable us to experience the grace, love, and power of God in ways that no other gift could. These weaknesses will be wrapped up with life, with immortality, and will persist as signs and amplifiers for the praise of the God who became weak but works with healing power through weakness for all eternity.

## Discussion Questions:

1. Read Revelation 22 slowly and carefully with your own image of the afterlife in mind. Where is that image confirmed in this chapter and where is it challenged or altered?
2. Read 2 Corinthians 4:7–5:10. How does Paul characterize this life? How does he characterize the next life? What are the connections between the two?
3. Do you believe our vision of the new heaven and new earth affects the decisions we make and the actions we take in the present? Describe a couple of practical ways this might affect us.
4. What personal weaknesses do you think will be done away with when you enter the next life? Which ones do you think will continue as signs of God's power and grace?

# 14

# Epilogue

As I complete the writing of this book Pascal is doing very well: his health is stable, he loves school, he is talking (and even writing) more and more, and his behavior continues to improve. Our family has found a new normal that incorporates Pascal's weaknesses, differences, and needs into a way of life we can all live together. We can go to church where Pascal knows the routine of the kindergarten class and children's church even if he is bigger than a lot of the kids. We have learned where we can go out to eat together, activities we can share, and how to balance and compromise in ways that help us get along and have fun together. It was not easy to get to this point, and I know that rocky roads may lie ahead. We are a few years away from facing puberty, which brings with it a host of maturity issues and often introduces bodily changes that can spark new seizures or other health problems in kids with Tuberous Sclerosis. We know God through the Spirit and our friends who follow Christ will continue to support and sustain us.

I hope this book has impacted you in a number of ways. I hope it has affected you emotionally, that you have had a taste of our feelings, and that it has expanded your compassion for families with special needs children and others who face a variety of difficult conditions. The stories of our family have given you, I hope, a window into our experiences, as stories have the power to evoke and

*Epilogue*

change our deepest emotional responses. I hope what I have written has changed the way you think, especially how you think about Scripture and weakness. We have looked in depth at a wide range of biblical passages that deal with the nature of creation, suffering and evil, healing and mercy, prophecy and justice, the identity of Jesus, the role of the Spirit, and God's renewal of all creation. You have probably encountered presentations and interpretations of Scripture that seem a bit different from what you already know. May this book give you a new love of Scripture and some new lenses for reading it well. Weakness is the thread that strings the book together from beginning to end, and weakness is a gift from God that has the ability to open us both to God's grace and power and to deeper relationships within the body of Christ. Finally, I hope this book has moved you to do something: to get to know a family with a special needs child, to make places for people with disabilities in your church, to welcome the weak and different into your own homes. Ultimately, I pray our own journey of following Christ while holding Pascal's hand may become your journey too as you walk the path of discipleship, holding the hand of and being held by someone who is weak and different.

# Bibliography and Suggestions for Further Reading

NOTE: THE FOLLOWING LIST identifies all of the materials cited in the footnotes of this book. These authors have enriched my own understanding of the intersection of disability, theology, and Scripture. I offer them here as suggestions for further reading on these topics.

Bakke, O. M. *When Children Became People: The Birth of Childhood in Early Christianity*. Translated by Brian McNeil. Minneapolis: Fortress, 2005.

Brueggemann, Walter. *The Prophetic Imagination*. 2nd ed. Minneapolis: Fortress, 2001.

Eiesland, Nancy L. *The Disabled God: Toward a Liberatory Theology of Disability*. Nashville: Abingdon, 1994.

Hauerwas, Stanley. *Suffering Presence: Theological Reflections on Medicine, the Mentally Handicapped, and the Church*. Notre Dame, IN: University of Notre Dame, 1986.

Hauerwas, Stanley, and Jean Vanier. *Living Gently in a Violent World: The Prophetic Witness of Weakness*. Resources for Reconciliation. Edited by Emmanuel Katangole and Chris Rice. Downers Grove, IL: InterVarsity, 2008.

Kierkegaard, Søren. *Purity of Heart Is to Will One Thing*. Translated by Douglas V. Steere. New York: HarperCollins, 1956.

Nouwen, Henri J. M. *Adam: God's Beloved*. Maryknoll, NY: Orbis, 2012.

Pohl, Christine D. *Making Room: Recovering Hospitality as a Christian Tradition*. Grand Rapids: Eerdmans, 1999.

Reynolds, Thomas E. *Vulnerable Communion: A Theology of Disability and Hospitality*. Grand Rapids: Brazos, 2008.

Vanier, Jean. *Becoming Human*. CBC Massey Lectures Series. Toronto: House of Anansi, 1998.

*Bibliography and Suggestions for Further Reading*

Yong, Amos. *The Bible, Disability, and the Church: A New Vision of the People of God*. Grand Rapids: Eerdmans, 2011.

———. *Theology and Down Syndrome: Reimagining Disability in Late Modernity*. Waco, TX: Baylor University Press, 2007

# Scripture Index

## Genesis

| | |
|---|---|
| 1:1 | 11 |
| 1:10 | 11 |
| 1:12 | 11 |
| 1:18 | 11 |
| 1:22 | 11 |
| 1:25 | 11 |
| 1:28 | 11, 73 |
| 1:31 | 11, 75 |
| 2:7 | 13 |
| 2:15 | 73 |
| 2:18 | 75 |
| 32:7 | 14 |

## Exodus

| | |
|---|---|
| 8:22 | 14 |
| 9:4 | 14 |
| 11:7 | 14 |
| 32:1–14 | 43 |
| 33:6 | 14 |
| 34:6 | 71, 77 |
| 34:7 | 77 |

## Leviticus

| | |
|---|---|
| 19:14 | 66 |

## Numbers

| | |
|---|---|
| 14:1–25 | 43 |

## Deuteronomy

| | |
|---|---|
| 10:18 | 4 |

## Judges

| | |
|---|---|
| 16 | 101 |

## 1 Samuel

| | |
|---|---|
| 13:14 | 92 |
| 16:1–2 | 88 |
| 16:6–7 | 87, 88 |
| 16:11 | 88 |
| 16:12 | 86 |
| 16:13 | 88 |
| 16:18 | 90 |
| 17 | 89 |
| 17:14–18 | 90 |
| 17:26–30 | 89 |
| 17:33 | 89 |
| 17:34–37 | 89 |
| 17:38–40 | 90 |
| 18:1–3 | 91 |
| 19:1–7 | 91 |

## Scripture Index

### 2 Samuel

| | |
|---|---|
| 6:14 | 90 |

### 2 Kings

| | |
|---|---|
| 10:4 | 14 |
| 20 | 63 |
| 22 | 59 |

### 1 Chronicles

| | |
|---|---|
| 15:16 | 90 |

### Job

| | |
|---|---|
| 1:4–5 | 35 |
| 1:8 | 35 |
| 2:3 | 35 |
| 2:11 | 30 |
| 2:12–13 | 31 |
| 4:5–6 | 34 |
| 8:2–6 | 34 |
| 11:2–6 | 35 |
| 16:1–3 | 32 |
| 18:2–4 | 35 |
| 18:5–6 | 34 |
| 42:3 | 34 |
| 42:7 | 32, 34–35 |
| 42:7–8 | XV, 34 |
| 42:8–9 | 35 |

### Psalms

| | |
|---|---|
| 4:3 | 14 |
| 7:11 | 60 |
| 11:7 | 60 |
| 13:2 | 92 |
| 13:5–6 | 92 |
| 17:7 | 14 |
| 31:1 | 60 |
| 32:3 | 92 |
| 32:11 | 92 |
| 72:2 | 60 |
| 112:1 | 14 |
| 139:1 | 12 |
| 139:2 | 12 |
| 139:3 | 12 |
| 139:4 | 12 |
| 139:6 | 14 |
| 139:8 | 12 |
| 139:9 | 12 |
| 139:12 | 12 |
| 139:14 | 10 |
| 139:13–16 | 12–14 |
| 139:18 | 13 |
| 139:19 | 14 |
| 139:24 | 14 |

### Proverbs

| | |
|---|---|
| 3:7 | 14 |
| 15:23 | 29 |
| 31:5 | 66 |
| 31:8 | 57, 66 |
| 31:9 | 60, 66, 72 |

### Ecclesiastes

| | |
|---|---|
| 1:2 | 21 |
| 1:3 | 21 |
| 2:14 | 21 |
| 3:1 | 20, 22 |
| 3:1–4 | 26 |
| 3:1–8 | 21–22 |
| 3:3 | 22 |
| 3:4 | 20, 22 |
| 3:8 | 22 |
| 3:14 | 22 |
| 4:9 | 22 |
| 5:1 | 22 |
| 5:7 | 22 |

*Scripture Index*

## Isaiah

| | |
|---|---|
| 6:1-5 | 44 |
| 11:6 | 79 |
| 45:8 | 60 |
| 53:5 | 42 |
| 58:6-7 | 61 |

## Jeremiah

| | |
|---|---|
| 2-3 | 59 |
| 4:5-31 | 59 |
| 4:19 | 43 |
| 7:1-10:16 | 59 |
| 10:17-25 | 59 |
| 7:16 | 43 |
| 8:22 | 38, 43-44 |
| 9:24 | 60 |
| 12:1-4 | 41 |
| 14:11 | 43 |
| 14:19-22 | 43 |
| 15:10-21 | 41 |
| 15:17 | 42 |
| 31:31-34 | 59 |
| 32:16-25 | 43 |
| 38:1-6 | 42 |

## Lamentations

| | |
|---|---|
| 1:1 | 42 |

## Hosea

| | |
|---|---|
| 3:1-5 | 44 |

## Amos

| | |
|---|---|
| 1-2 | 59 |
| 2:6-8 | 44 |
| 2:7 | 66 |
| 5:10-11 | 66 |
| 5:12 | 66 |
| 5:24 | 60 |
| 7:14 | 59 |

## Micah

| | |
|---|---|
| 7:9 | 60 |

## Zechariah

| | |
|---|---|
| 1:1 | 44 |
| 4:6 | 90 |
| 7:10 | 4 |

## Malachi

| | |
|---|---|
| 1:2-3 | 38, 42 |
| 1:4-5 | 42 |

## Matthew

| | |
|---|---|
| 5:3 | 72, 81, 104 |
| 6:33 | 60 |
| 10:30 | 12 |
| 12:43-45 | 54 |
| 17:14-21 | 47 |
| 18:1-5 | 106-107 |
| 18:1-14 | 9 |
| 18:4 | 84 |
| 18:5 | 1, 64 |
| 18:6 | 64 |
| 18:6-7 | 106 |
| 18:10 | 106 |
| 18:14 | 106 |
| 25:14-30 | 110 |
| 25:19 | 110 |
| 25:21 | 111 |
| 25:23 | 111 |
| 26:41 | 101 |

# Scripture Index

## Mark

| | |
|---|---|
| 1:25 | 53 |
| 1:34 | 53 |
| 1:41 | 52 |
| 2:8 | 50 |
| 5:8 | 53 |
| 6:13 | 53 |
| 6:34 | 52 |
| 7:32–34 | 56 |
| 8:2 | 52 |
| 8:22–10:52 | 48 |
| 8:31 | 55 |
| 8:33 | 48 |
| 9:14–16 | 48 |
| 9:14–29 | 46–47, 77 |
| 9:16 | 48 |
| 9:17–18 | 48 |
| 9:21 | 49 |
| 9:22 | 47–48, 50, 52, 55 |
| 9:23 | 52, 55 |
| 9:25 | 50, 53 |
| 9:25–27 | 53 |
| 9:26 | 52 |
| 9:28–29 | 48, 55 |
| 9:30–32 | 104 |
| 9:33–37 | 104 |
| 9:38–39 | 48 |
| 9:42 | 104 |
| 10:1–12 | 105 |
| 10:13–14 | 48 |
| 10:13–16 | 107 |
| 10:14 | 104 |
| 10:15 | 105 |
| 10:20 | 105 |
| 10:22 | 105 |
| 10:27 | 105 |
| 10:32–34 | 104 |
| 10:42–45 | 48 |
| 11:20 | 48 |
| 14:28 | 55 |

## Luke

| | |
|---|---|
| 1:58 | 97 |
| 1:78 | 52, 96 |
| 2 | 59 |
| 4:18–21 | 4 |
| 6:21 | 20, 27 |
| 6:20–23 | 28 |
| 6:35 | 98 |
| 6:36 | 94, 97–98 |
| 6:37 | 97 |
| 9:37–43 | 47 |
| 10:37 | 97 |
| 11:24–26 | 54 |
| 14:13–14 | 98 |
| 18:29–30 | 6 |
| 22:26 | 84 |
| 24:39 | 112 |
| 24:40 | 16 |

## John

| | |
|---|---|
| 17:5 | 10 |
| 17:26 | 95 |
| 20:26–29 | 112 |
| 20:27 | 16 |

## Acts

| | |
|---|---|
| 1:11 | 110 |
| 14:22 | 111 |
| 17:31 | 60 |

## Romans

| | |
|---|---|
| 1:17 | 60 |
| 1:18 | 60 |
| 3:25–26 | 60 |
| 6:4–5 | 112 |
| 8:20–22 | 109 |
| 8:26 | 113 |
| 8:29 | 114 |
| 8:30 | 114 |
| 12:6 | 59 |
| 12:21 | 70, 77 |

*Scripture Index*

## 1 Corinthians

| | |
|---|---|
| 1:18–2:5 | 107 |
| 1:27 | 88 |
| 2:3 | 103 |
| 2:4–5 | 103 |
| 7:27–29 | 110 |
| 12:10 | 59 |
| 12:21–23 | 106 |
| 13 | 106 |
| 15:43 | 113 |
| 15:44 | 113 |
| 15:53–54 | 113 |

## 2 Corinthians

| | |
|---|---|
| 4:7 | 113 |
| 4:7–5:10 | 115 |
| 5:1 | 113 |
| 5:4 | 113 |
| 12:9 | 101 |

## Galatians

| | |
|---|---|
| 4:13–14 | 102 |

## Ephesians

| | |
|---|---|
| 1:4 | 10 |

## Philippians

| | |
|---|---|
| 2:1 | 96 |
| 2:6–11 | 111 |

## Colossians

| | |
|---|---|
| 3:1 | 112 |
| 3:12 | 96 |

## 2 Thessalonians

| | |
|---|---|
| 1:5 | 60 |

## Titus

| | |
|---|---|
| 1:1–3 | 10 |

## Hebrews

| | |
|---|---|
| 8 | 59 |
| 12:12 | 101 |

## James

| | |
|---|---|
| 2:1–7 | 63 |
| 2:5 | 4 |
| 2:13 | 77 |

## 1 Peter

| | |
|---|---|
| 1:3 | 97 |
| 2:21 | 112 |

## 1 John

| | |
|---|---|
| 3:10 | 60 |
| 4:7 | 77 |
| 4:9–10 | 71 |
| 4:18 | 77 |

## Revelation

| | |
|---|---|
| 4 | 16 |
| 5:5–6 | 72 |
| 5:6 | 16 |
| 7:9–10 | 112 |
| 13:9–10 | 76 |
| 14:12–13 | 76 |
| 19:9 | 76 |
| 20:7–10 | 16 |

## Scripture Index

### Revelation *(continued)*

| | |
|---|---|
| 21:4 | 17 |
| 21:1–8 | 17 |
| 21:4 | 113 |
| 21:9 | 76 |
| 21:9–10 | 17 |
| 21:22–27 | 17 |
| 22 | 115 |
| 22:1–2 | 114 |
| 22:2 | 17, 109 |
| 22:5 | 112 |

www.ingramcontent.com/pod-product-compliance
Lightning Source LLC
Chambersburg PA
CBHW072154160426
43197CB00012B/2381